FINDING
(and keeping)
YOUR STAR
RECRUITS
IN JAPAN

Tips from an expert
who has interviewed
more than 10,000 people

Guide for HR
professionals
and job seekers

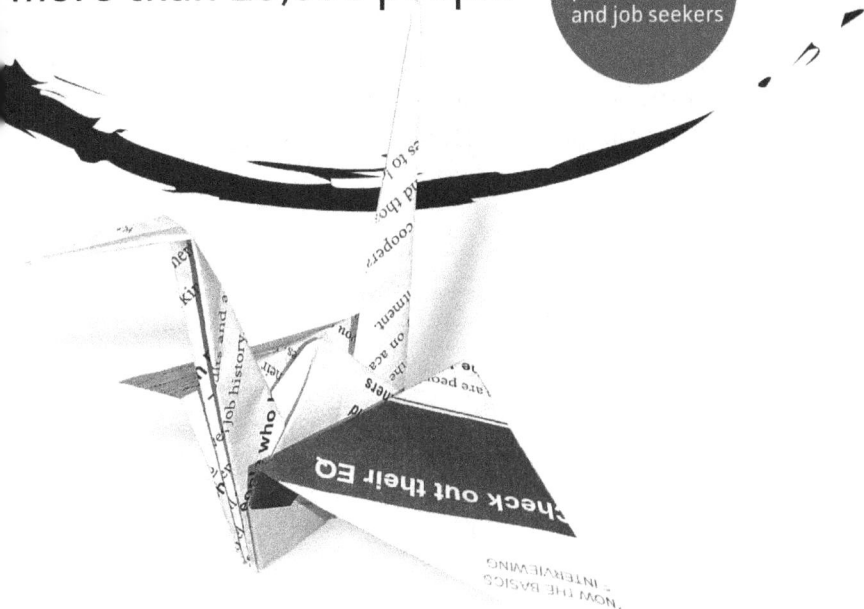

Kenichiro Yadokoro

Sougansha

Sougansha Paperback

Finding (and keeping)
YOUR STAR RECRUITS IN JAPAN

Tips from an expert who has interviewed more than 10,000 people

English translation © 2016 by Sougansha
Author: Kenichiro Yadokoro

First published in Japan 2014 with the title *Yoi jinzai wo minuku SAIYOU MENSETSU POINT*, copyright © Kenichiro Yadokoro 2014 by KEIEISHOIN, SANRO Research Institute, Inc.

ISBN 978-4-908521-13-3
Sougansha Paperbacks are edited and published by Sougansha.
Saegusa Bldg. Yoyogiko-en 3rd Fl., 1-7-20 Uehara, Shibuya-ku, Tokyo, Japan 151-0064

Permission:
This book is translated from Japanese into English. There is no consideration for the cultural differences between these two countries.

INTRODUCTION

Every recruit for every job helps build the foundations of a company. Every recruitment decision is vital because a single bad decision can harm the company.

I have been involved in recruiting men and women for more than twenty years, and have interviewed more than ten thousand candidates for Japanese Companies. There were occasions when I was forced to make compromises because of a dearth of applicants. These people rarely lasted long.

Many recruiters find it hard to look their candidates in the eye, especially when interviewing for senior executive positions or human resources staff. They feel intimidated. Others have difficulty figuring out what type of person their company is after. These people struggle to keep an ace workforce.

Applicants come, hoping for a job. They try to present themselves in the most appealing way possible. They have an answer prepared for every question. They have rehearsed their reasons for applying a million times. It is not a hard decision at all if the interviewee means what they say. However, if the candidate stages an award-winning deception during the interview, they may deceive the interviewer and get the job but later be labeled as "useless" by the area they are assigned to—and the recruiter can expect to receive complaints.

To pick a good apple, recruiters must learn the art of scrutiny. If they rely on their personal preferences, or if they decide to swallow whole an applicant's well-rehearsed answers without analysis, the chances are high that they will never find "the one" for the job.

In this book, I shall share my recruiting and interviewing skills to help recruiters find the right staff.

The first rule to finding the right person is, of course, to be the right company for the applicant. The right company will attract the right candidates. Without the right candidates, it is impossible to find the right person. Even if you spot a gem, an unofficial offer would not be enough to keep them if they are simply not interested in your company. Keep in mind that it is not only we, the company, who are making choices. The applicants are also choosing the company to work for and comparing your company with others.

The second rule to finding the right person is to be a "people person." Companies that see labor as "human resources" and "human capital" grow and prosper; those that simply fire everyone who seem to be of no use to them end up recruiting often, and losing both money and time. Labor is not a commodity. People think, feel, and dream. Doing well in school or scoring high in written examinations does not equate to being a great worker. Candidates need to be studied to determine if they are worth an offer. Simply complaining that you never seem to recruit the right people is not good enough.

It would be my pleasure to know if the skills and tips in this book help you find your perfect match.

Best wishes,
Kenichiro Yadokoro

Table of contents

CHAPTER 2
SCRUTINIZE THE APPLICATION

Column 2

CHAPTER 3
KNOW THE BASICS OF INTERVIEWING

Column 3

CHAPTER 4
FIND THE TRUTH BEHIND ACTIONS
AND ATTITUDES

Column 4

CHAPTER 5
ASK THE STANDARD QUESTIONS

Column 5

CHAPTER 6
ASK MORE SPECIFIC QUESTIONS

CHAPTER 9
HELPFUL DOCUMENTS

CHAPTER 1

REVIEW YOUR RECRUITMENT SYSTEM

Recruiting seems to be a very simple process. A candidate applies for the job and survives the recruitment process, and all you have to do is decide if they get the job or not. It may seem simple, but if you're not finding good workers, it's time to pause and reconsider your processes.

1 Send out a strong message

We seek reasons and solutions right away when we see sales figures drop, but when it comes to recruitment we tend to give excuses, such as "There were no good applicants this year." Could it be that the good applicants found your company not of interest to them, and went to other companies?

I once had a manager friend consult me about why not many people had showed up at the company's recruitment information session that year. As I learned more about the situation, I discovered that the ad posted for the information session had been a template message that merely gave the date and venue—nothing more. It seems the HR person in charge of writing tailored introductions to recruitment advertisements had resigned and everyone was too busy to fill the gap. A template message was used instead. I rewrote the advertisement immediately. I outlined what the company did and included the CEO's comments about the company's future. I also advised my friend to ask the CEO to give a presentation at the information session and to make sure that everyone knew he was appearing. The result?—twice the number of attendees at their next information session than ever before.

Candidates look at companies more closely and cautiously than any HR professional would ever imagine, sieving out the companies that don't interest them. To recruit the right candidates, you must first catch their eye. It is not enough to use information sessions and recruitment ads alone. It is important to also use media such as SNS and the company homepage to draw their attention. Don't just talk about your company's rosy future. Give candidates a glimpse of what your company is like now, including exactly what your current employees do. This helps the candidates visualize working in your company. If you can't make the candidates feel excited about you, it is likely that you won't be their first choice, even if they do apply.

A manager of a small food company asked for my advice on recruiting undergrads as well as graduates from high school. Given the company's out-of-the-way location, I could see that they would need to do more than just rely on recruitment ads. I suggested that their ads could be fewer but punchier—they needed something else that would grab the attention of the students. So they cut their advertisement budget by half, and allocated the money to sending new recruits overseas to learn about food culture. After they sent word out about this intention, a surprising number of applications were received and the company easily managed to recruit its target number. Therefore, it is very important to add a punch to your ads—preferably something you can build on throughout the long recruitment process.

Don't complain about not being able to recruit the right people if you haven't tried to put out a strong, clear and precise message to them. If you fail to put yourself in the applicants' shoes, it is unlikely that you'll get any applicants.

2 Revitalize your processes

Whether you are recruiting fresh graduates or mid-career applicants, the recruitment process starts when you are strategizing your advertising for a job position—and it *do*es not finish until the successful applicants have settled down in your company. It is disturbing the number of HR people who think that recruiting is just about deciding if the applicant gets the job or not. To me, it is not until the applicant becomes a fully integrated part of the workforce that recruitment ends. The applicants know the company through the HR staff, and they choose to accept their job offer based on the trust they feel for the recruiting personnel. If we just decide to leave it all to their allocated departments or work areas, and that it is none of our business anymore, the new recruits will feel disappointed and maybe even let down.

Recruitment tests such as interviews are an essential and well-known part of the recruiting process. **Yet sometimes applicants are confused about what is involved.** For example, they might say, "The ad stated that candidates would go through up to three interviews, but an offer was made only after one interview." The ad has not lied—"up to three" can mean just one, but the implication in the ad is that there would be at least two interviews. You might decide that there is nothing wrong with making an early offer, but be aware that your decision could cause doubts to arise in the minds of applicants who receive an offer. They are not sure if you have made your decision based on a proper understanding of them, or if you have just offered the job to anyone who was available. A small point, perhaps, but it could nonetheless shake their confidence in your company and make them hesitate about accepting your offer (especially if they are receiving other offers).

On the other hand, there are companies who spend months recruiting people, from receiving applications to making the final decisions. This can be hard on candidates, especially if they are out of work. Of course, they can always give the company a call to check on the progress of their application, but be aware that most candidates will not do this for fear that it could make them appear impatient or bullying, and thus affect the outcome.

There are also companies that interview their applicants over and over again. By forcing the applicant to repeat their reasons for applying again and again, the applicants can get fed up and lose their motivation to work in the company. Those who just interview for the sake of it will never be able to discover the candidates' potential: they only know how to repeat their questions.

So what is a good recruitment time span? For fresh grads, it should not take more than a month from the final interview to making offers. For mid-career recruitments, it should only take 2–3 weeks. There should be no more than three interviews, and the applicants should be closely observed throughout each interview (see Chapter 3). If you drag out the process, you might end up losing your potential workers to other companies who get their offers in before you.

The recruitment process

Strategizing → advertising → receiving applications → recruitment paperwork → interviews → deciding on whom to hire → making an informal offer → following up → informal training (optional) → hiring preparation → entry to the company → training → allocation to department → follow-ups after the allocation

3 Think about the characteristics of your applicants

People nowadays tend to search for a job based on practical considerations rather than the desire to find their "dream job." They are interested in the working conditions and whether the company is stable. **If you think you don't need to compromise to suit their needs, you are unlikely to get the right people. Keep in mind that you have to be chosen in order to choose.**

With no experience in the field, fresh grads tend to prioritize the companies they know. There are also students that don't have a clue what they want to do but know they want to "look good" in the eyes of society. Universities now offer courses on job-hunting, starting from year 1. There are also places that offer to help job seekers for a fee. As a result, more and more students arrive fully prepared with their practiced entry sheets and trained interview skills. In these cases, the applicants' practical ability, working potential, and eagerness to enter the company are important factors to consider when deciding to make an offer. A good strategy for fresh grads is to use the information session and recruitment process to reinforce their affection for the company. It is important to appeal to applicants' emotions while at the same time studying them closely. Some interviewers claim that there are interviewees who come lacking research in the field and in their company. However, this ignorance may be more the fault of an inadequate, non-engaging information session. It is not fair to have high expectations of students who lack work experience. It is the job of HR to inform them of what they should do while keeping their motivation high throughout the recruitment process.

Mid-career applicants have experience in the workforce, whether short or long. These applicants want to avoid making the same mistakes they made in their former workplace, thus they are more likely to be careful regarding the working conditions and wages your company has to offer. When it comes to mid-career recruits, it is not just about the applicants' passion—their working ability and work readiness are also important criteria for their employment. Within the short timeframe of an interview, it is critical to discover if a mid-career applicant is work-ready and has attained the requisite skills.

Some currently employed applicants apply in the hope of better working conditions and are willing to change jobs if they receive a good-enough offer. These applicants may be vague about when they can join your company, and may turn down an offer. If you believe that they are your desired recruits, you will need to beat what their current job has to offer in order to encourage them to make the switch.

When recruiting mid-career, bear in mind that what is written on the résumé and what is answered during the interview may not always be the same. Applicants may highlight even the shortest work experiences in the hope of a job. To prevent mismatching, it is essential that you ask concrete questions during the interview about the applicant's job skills.

4 Review your working environment

Many companies, even small ones, tend to judge their workers by their graduated university or former workplace—the more prestigious the university or the more renowned the company, the more attractive is the applicant. However, if your workplace isn't fit for such star recruits, it will not attract them. Check if your company's working environment is ready. Problems found must be resolved. If your working environment is not good enough to attract workers from first-class universities and first-class companies, the quality of the workers you are able to recruit will be limited.

It may be costly to maintain a good working environment, but it is worth considering when you think of the brilliant staff you may acquire. So before you rejoice about the high standard of your applicants, review your working environment to see if it is compatible with those standards. If the company is not ready enough, the new recruits will not stay.

At the same time, do not judge a book by its cover.

5 Do not judge a book by its cover

When recruiting for graduate positions, it is certainly hard not to refer to their graduated university. After all, they have no former workplace. However, it is also essential to look into their reasons for applying to your company.

For mid-career recruits, it is their working skills that you should be focusing on, not their job and academic history. Try not to be influenced by their academic profile and the name of their former employer. Base your judgment on whether they are job-ready and whether they have the requisite skills. The circumstances of your company must be explained to them and they must understand what they would be expected to do in the company, if selected.

Even when recruiting managers, an impressive title on their résumé does not mean they are able to take an active part in your company. Recruiting with the vague hope that such an applicant will make your company a better place could backfire. Your star recruit might end up resigning because they cannot get along with the rest of the crew.

Be specific about your hopes and expectations when

giving an offer. Do not let presentation or credentials deceive you. Although you should give applicants full credit for having graduated from a first-class university, or for having worked in a top company, the past is the past and should only be considered as a small part of who the applicant is now.

When recruiting for mid-career positions, many companies sieve out applicants during the screening process who have changed jobs frequently or have a long blank period on their résumé. This is a mistake. Unless they are clearly not suitable, you should judge only after seeing them at an interview. A friend of mine changed jobs so frequently in his 20s he could hardly get a job. He is now working for an A-listed company. There are people in this world who are willing to give their all for the company that was willing to take them on, despite the negative of having a blank period on their résumé or an unsettled work history. **A person's past is a good indicator, but it is not all. Without an objective frame of mind, wrong judgments can be made.**

Indeed, there are companies so committed to finding the right fit for their company that they accept graduate applicants with the name of their university unrevealed.

6 Know your company well

You need to know your company well in order not to be distracted by an applicant's academic profile or job history during the recruitment process. This means knowing the characteristics of the people or working frameworks that result in high achievement (competency model), which of course differs between careers and companies. Try looking at current employees of your company who achieved high within five years of joining you. By analyzing their characteristics, you might find similar traits, which you can then look for in your recruits. This strategy will help you find the right fit.

For example, you could conduct an aptitude test of existing staff and analyze the traits for high achievers from the test results. If you find common traits—such as willingness to take on challenges, tolerance to high pressure, good communication skills—you will have found the traits to look for in you applicants during recruitment.

Of course, don't make you decision based merely on data. Try hearing from the managers of the departments and work areas, and see what they think. You might learn something new. As an example, if one of the desired traits is "not using negative terms while speaking," ask the applicant about times when they feel they might have failed to do this. Applicants that are able to learn from their failures, instead of blaming others, have matched up with your competency.

Let employees who have worked for three to five years in your company participate in information sessions. The fresh grads seldom picture themselves ten or twenty years on. They tend to imagine themselves in just a few years' time. Even with passion and will, without understanding the reality of the company, applicants may not end up becoming good workers. And if you simply judge a person by their words, there is a chance that their actions may not follow their words. By analyzing the characteristics of a good workforce and listing the traits to look for, you are able to reduce the chances of mismatching during recruitment.

If you look at your company's competency model and the applicant doesn't fit 100%, you will be able to glean what the applicant is lacking and ask about their weaknesses during an interview. By knowing your company's competency well, you can focus on those points when writing up the recruitment ad. For example, if communication skills are a must, they should be listed in the ad as a "must-have skill."

Recruitment is not about getting enough heads—

it's about finding the right people for your company.
Therefore, it is crucial that you know the characteristics of those who are doing well and recruit people who have similar characteristics to join your workforce.

Examples of competency:

- Good communication skills
- Able to take responsibility
- Willing to take on challenges
- Able to accomplish tasks
- Goal-oriented
- Stress-tolerant
- Able to work with others
- Consistent

7 Know what makes your company stand out from others

Recruitment is a battle with other companies. Check on the recruitment ads from the same field. If you find points you could polish in your own ads, do so immediately.

To find the right recruits, you need to know what makes your company stand out from others. But it doesn't help if you are the only one who knows what this is. Applicants are attracted to the strengths and reputation of a company, which is why they put in an application in the first place. If you're not getting the right people, the chances are you haven't advertised your strengths well enough to job hunters.

Some HR staff stress the gravitas of the company during information sessions and interviews, but this does not necessarily appeal to applicants. It does not help them picture their future selves. Instead, the elites choose other companies.

Be creative. You need to have something that other companies don't have.

When I was involved in recruitment in the beauty industry, companies battled with each other to attract elite beauticians. This industry is labor-intensive. It cannot afford to stop work to recruit staff—even if they put out an 'open' sign, there is no way a beauty salon can run without its staff. Thus our strategy to victory was to increase the daily working hours in exchange for three days off per week. There were many companies who didn't even offer two days off per week, so we were very attractive to job hunters. As a result, we received a load of applications and were able to find the perfect people.

Even if there are downfalls and negatives in your company, you can reassure the applicant by presenting your improvement strategy during information sessions and interviews. Applicants tend to have empathy for a company if its problems are linked to future development.

Just complaining about not having any competitive strength over other companies does not attract job hunters.

The strengths of your company can be demonstrated by listing its characteristics. If you have fine products or technology, for example, this can attract some applicants. While presenting your company's characteristics (i.e. the points that make you stand out from other companies), increase the credibility of your list by adding examples. Job hunters' interest may be piqued after reading your list. They will want to learn more about you.

It is the interviewers that present the strengths and future of the company to the applicants who have the power to move the applicants and influence their decision to work for the company.

Know your strengths:

- Characteristics of your products
- Superiority
- Sales
- Ordinary profit
- Position in the field
- Stability of workforce
- Working environment
- Average wage
- New industries

Become an interviewer who can talk about your company's present and future:

- Understand the sales, ordinary profit, stated capital, capital-to-asset ratio, market share, and more about your company
- Present the plans for new industries and the overall future plan for your company in as much detail as you are allowed to

8 Be aggressive during recruitment

Aggressive recruitment means passionately promoting the strengths of your company in the hope of more applications. Applicants don't just show up after a recruitment ad is posted. To find the right person for the job, you need to make sure your message has gotten through to the job hunters. You need to strategize to get more applicants. If you don't get good quality applications, revise your ad or where it has been posted. Re-examine what you are doing to maximize your ad.

Just setting up a booth in joint information sessions may fail to draw the attention of job hunters. Put up punchy posters, or other media, or make use of your current workers—those who are at a similar age to your targeted job hunters—by getting them to participate in information sessions (or in any other way). Do all you can to grasp the attention of suitable job hunters.

Job hunters are given a good impression when they see the whole company involved in passionate recruitment for a good workforce. So, if possible, get the CEO or department managerial staff to be involved in the recruitment process too. **Companies that involve their managerial staff in recruitment activities tend to value their staff. Their involvement impresses not only potential new recruits, but current staff as well.** Create a recruitment system that not only involves HR but other employees from other departments of the company.

Just revising the recruitment process or the recruitment ad isn't enough. It is important that you get rid of the "Thank me for hiring you" sort of mindset and strategize to sway job hunters into your field.

To recruit experienced workers, you can find your target in various ways, including employment agencies, staffing agencies, headhunting, etc. Recruitment sites offer a scout function that allows companies to approach job hunters instead of just waiting for job hunters to come to them.

Recruitment is similar to sales. Products rarely sell just by sitting there. Sales grow according to the advertising strategy. The products are advertised so that the consumers can see their best aspects and thus be persuaded to buy the product. Recruiters persuade job hunters into working for them by strategizing their advertisements and presenting their best side to the job hunters.

Some companies use recruitment agencies to double-check their promotional work. It helps also to use up-to-date tools such as SNS sites because this will bring you closer to the job hunters that are likely to be using social media. Other good ideas are to have a recruitment system within your company, or approach schools where the children of your existing workers attend, or approach their alma maters.

Nowadays, globalization is a very big topic. With more and more companies in need of a foreign workforce, it may be necessary to start strategizing for overseas recruits.

Being aggressive during recruitment:

- Use new media to reach your target audience
- Use the scout function to approach job hunters through recruitment sites
- Work on your booth's presentation during events in order to attract job hunters
- Create an inner recruitment system or introductory system

9   Determine whom you should (and should not) hire

Recruitment personnel need to know whom they should take on and whom they should not. If they fail to do so, recruitment is reduced to a mere gamble. **People— regardless of whether they are new graduates or mid-career applicants—should be hired because of their high potentiality. They should have the type of skills and knowledge that the company can utilize.** Conversely, the applicants you should stay away from are the ones that not only lack the requisite standard for the job, but also lack passion and will.

It may be difficult to decide who is the best person for the job, but it is crucial that you weed out those who are clearly not suitable. Even with superior ability, people who fail to consider others mess up the team if they are employed. On the other hand, people who move only to others' orders may get in the way of the company's growth and mess up the working atmosphere.

Some people own irrelevant certificates or diplomas. It is likely that these people haven't decided on their career yet. Even if you employ them, they may not stay for long. Without knowing the applicant and deciding to hire them based just on their ability, or because they seem okay increases the risks of mismatching during recruitment. Therefore, it is crucial that you are able to define people you should be hiring and those whom you should not.

Applicants you should consider hiring:

- High working potential
- Have the required skills, knowledge and experience
- Conscious about problem solving and take action
- Work constructively
- Able to see another's point of view
- Learn from their mistakes
- Able to work with others
- Keep promises
- Keep going and never give up
- High concentration
- Understand your business concept
- Can establish their career vision in your company
- Can self-analyze
- Have a strong will to work for your company and know what they are doing

Applicants you should stay away from:

- Dishonest
- Rationalize all their actions
- Don't fit in the workforce
- Have problems with their working abilities
- Not willing to work
- Break promises
- Short in passion and will towards working for the company
- Don't listen
- There is a duality in action
- Low working potential
- Take things negatively
- Not willing to improve
- Lack understanding of the company and in general
- Lost about what they should do
- Brag a lot

10 Give the recruitment staff a common purpose

When interviews are conducted with multiple HR staff present, it is essential to reach consensus before any final decision is made. If the decision is made purely on the interviewer's likes and dislikes or feelings, it is likely that you have not recruited the best people. Make sure all the recruitment staff share the same understanding of the aim of the recruitment and know which kind of person they are looking for. For this reason, meetings before the interview are essential, especially when recruitment is based on a single interview, or when other departments are in charge.

Recruitment is all about team play. The recruitment procedures should be explained to all the recruitment staff, even if they are not conducting the interview. In this way, you will be able to learn about the behavior of applicants at reception and in the waiting room, not just during the interview. It all adds up to building a complete picture of each applicant. **By giving a common purpose to the recruitment staff, you will be able to picture clearly what type of person you are looking for.**

Another advantage to having multiple staff members in

charge of recruitment is that they can hone their interview skills by conducting mock interviews. The ones who play the interviewee's part in the mock interview learn how the interviewee feels. They may then put their understanding and empathy into practice during real interviews.

A further advantage is that when an interviewer is unsure of a decision, they can always refer to other interviewers for advice. Staff can also work on the common knowledge stated in a pre-interview checklist created beforehand (see template next page.).

Pre-interview checklist template

Explaining the strengths and attractive features of the company

-
-

The company's weaknesses and plans for improvement

-
-

Aim of the recruitment

-
-

Details of the job description for the specific job listing

-
-

Characteristics of the ideal candidate

-
-

Skills and experience required

-
-

The recruitment process (interview dates, schedule from unofficial offer to joining the company)

-
-

Column 1

Attract interest of job hunters through events

Many companies set up a booth in recruitment events and introduce their company to job hunters. However, there are booths that attract people and some that do not. The popularity of the type of job does have an influence on the results, but it is not the only factor influencing the result. Try to set up a display that is eye-catching, and let staff in the same age group as the job hunters join in. The displays show the uniqueness and characteristics of your company, while the presence of existing employees serves as a visual cue to the applicants, helping them imagine themselves working for your company. If you are able to approach, do not just sit there—try to engage with passers-by. If the HR department has given up on attracting job hunters, the job hunters will definitely know.

Please think about how you will tell others about the attractive features of your company.

CHAPTER 2

SCRUTINIZE
THE APPLICATION

An applicant's written application —consisting of résumé, and either an entry sheet (fresh grads), or a CV (mid-career recruits)— plays a large part in determining if they are right for your workforce. However, without the skills to check whether what is written is true, it is impossible to really know the applicant. As most interviews are based on the written application, scrutinizing these documents correctly is essential to finding the right person for the job.

1 Points in the résumé you should verify

From applicants' résumés, you should be able to see their reasons for applying, their career aims and their working skills. If the terms desired from the applicant differ from what the company has to offer, they may have to be turned down, even if otherwise a great candidate.

When perusing the application, note the small details as well—for example, if the applicant's address is a long way away, transport may become an issue.

If you find the applicant has qualifications in fields completely irrelevant to the advertised job, your job may not be the applicant's dream job. Alternatively, the applicant might be a "qualifications maniac" who prioritizes their self-development in areas irrelevant to the position.

If the résumé is handwritten, you may also gain insight into the type of person they are and their degree of interest in your company. It is not their handwriting per se that you should focus on. Rather, if the résumé is carefully written, we can expect the applicant to be a careful worker. (The same can be said of typed résumés—a neat layout and the absence of typos show that the applicant has taken care.)

For those who have chosen to structure their own résumé instead of using a standard template, make sure you ask in the interview about the points they didn't include—because they may be only including what is favorable to them.

Checkpoints for the résumé

Checkpoints	
The applicant's eyes are dull in their application photo.	
The address is not fully filled in.	
No landline phone is recorded.	
The name of the school/company is not recorded.	
The year of entry and/or the year of graduation incorrect.	
There is a blank period of more than six months with no explanation.	
There are multiple qualifications in multiple areas.	
Applicant is pursuing (or has pursued) a professional career.	
Address a long way away—applicant may lack transport to get to the workplace.	
Applicant uncompromising on desired terms.	
Applicant has not used the résumé template.	
Intentions of entry are too generic (not targeted at the company).	
Presentation is vague.	
All interests are listed regardless of relevance.	
The reasons for leaving former workplaces are all given as "personal reasons."	

X would be a potentially problematic factor that you need to consider.

	Working ability	Desire to join the company	Willingness to work	Stability
		X	X	
	X	X		
			X	X
	X	X	X	
	X			X
				X
				X
		X		X
	X	X	X	
	X	X		X
		X		
		X		X
	X	X		
			X	X
	X			X

(1) The address not fully filled in and other missing details

One of the easy spots to miss when skimming through a résumé is the applicant's address. Check that the applicant has given their complete address. It may seem a small point—the address given may be sufficient to find them—but **just by checking if the address is fully provided you can assess how keen the person is to make a good first impression.** An incomplete address could indicate a worker who rushes through their work without much care. Make sure you check on this during the interview. Applicants who have been turned down continuously tend to write and send as many résumés as they can, and speed can result in the omission of words in their résumé.

Some applicants use abbreviations for the names of schools and companies mentioned on their résumé. Once again, this could indicate sloppiness or disinterest. During the interview, you should check their level of interest in working for your company.

The address block should be at the top of the résumé, whether printed or handwritten. Look deeper than the document, try to grasp the applicant's thoughts.

Things to look out for:

- Does the paperwork indicate attention to detail?
- Are there signs that the applicant has been turned down many times, resulting in a sloppy résumé?

(2) The year of entry and year of graduation mistaken

Check on the entry and graduation years listed. If the years recorded are mistaken, it's also likely that the following job experience records will also be incorrect. If it is just a slip, it can be easily fixed by asking the applicant to resubmit a corrected résumé. However, it could be intentional.

Usually, applicants would have been 13 years old when they entered secondary school, 16 when they entered high school, and 19 when they were accepted into a university. Check the years of entry and years of graduation just in case. Those who make such mistakes tend to lack concentration and might end up triggering huge problems in your company.

If you find a mistake, point it out to the applicant—their reaction will show you their style of working. **Those who quickly apologize and re-submit a corrected résumé will be good at following-up their work, but those who give you excuses may lack a sense of**

responsibility and the potential to improve.

Things to look out for:

- -

- Is there a lack of concentration?
- Is there a tendency to rush and makes assumptions?

(3) Pencil marks on the margins of the résumé

Check to see if the résumé is clean or not. It is costly to get turned down continuously, so instead of submitting a new résumé for each job, some applicants re-send older, unsuccessful résumés. If you find one with a rubbed off 'X' mark, or with an old date, it could be a re-used résumé. These applicants will not have targeted their application to suit your company. It is also likely that they lack working ability, so you should be careful when deciding to hire them.

There are many applicants who lose their passion, and even start to lose trust in companies, through continuous turndowns. They apply with an attitude of "I'm not going to get the job anyway." **Those who recycle résumés may be messy in their work practices, and not giving their best.** Those who sincerely want the job will take care of their documents so they are sent properly without leaving unsightly folding marks. It is not just the content of the résumé but its date and condition that can give you a glimpse of how the applicant works.

Things to look out for:

- Does the résumé appear recycled? This could be due to continuous turndowns from other companies.
- Is the résumé sloppy? This could indicate the applicant has no serious desire to work.

(4) Uncompromising on desired terms

Those applicants who fixate on wages and conditions at the application stage may only be interested in the terms being offered. Those who are stubborn about their starting wage may lack self-confidence. **Their fear is that they are unlikely to get promoted; therefore, they need to get as much as they can at the start.**

The time for discussing a starting wage and working conditions is during the interview, but their lack of self-confidence makes them state everything in advance in the written application. These people—those who apply simply because of the terms offered—will change jobs once they are given a better offer. Therefore, you should check on their future plans and working attitude during the interview.

Over-confidence can also be a problem. Those who ask for more than what the recruitment ad has stated may not work out well with the existing staff. It would not be good for the workforce if the new recruit, even one that had experience, lacked humility as the new kid on the block.

Even if you fulfill their wishes, those who dwell on wages and conditions will just ask for more once they join your company. Think twice before making your decision.

Things to look out for:

- Is the applicant fixated on their desired terms (a sign of a lack of confidence)?
- Is the applicant likely to change jobs based on the terms offered instead of the work itself?

(5) Intentions of entry that are not meant for your company

The entry-intention column reflects the applicant's understanding of the particular job and their intentions towards the company itself. It is also one of the ways you can see if your company is the applicant's first choice. **When applicants' intentions of entry are based only on the current condition of the company, they may be self-centered applicants who lack the will to contribute to the company.** If the applicants show their willingness to contribute to the company based on previous experience, and state the reasons for applying to your company (out of all the other companies out there), you can assume that your company is their first choice and can expect them to contribute to the company.

Those who experience continuous turndowns from companies tend to get lazy about researching a company's background. They write entry intentions that would fit any company. Be sure to question their reasons for applying to your company over others during the interview.

When mid-career recruitment applications don't match their original work type, there is a chance that these applicants lack the stability to work continuously for the same company.

There are also applicants that fill in every blank, giving far too much information, much of it irrelevant. These applicants tend to assume things and may not be a good match for your company, though you may not find this out until after they join. Reveal the unvarnished truth about the job (its difficulties and drawbacks) during the interview and see how they react.

Things to look out for:

- Are there vague intentions of entry, signaling that you are not their first choice?

- Is the applicant fixated on the glamorous aspects of the company? They may lack staying power if the reality does not match the dream.

Hence, by questioning the claims on the résumé, you are able to build an accurate and fair picture of each applicant. You need to do the same with regard to the entry sheet and CV.

(6) The applicant's eyes are dull in their photo

The applicant's passion and willingness to work can be gleaned from the photo on their résumé. You can say the same about interviews—applicants who present as energetic tend to be confident and passionate about their work. Conversely, those who present in a lackluster way, including in the snapshot they have provided, may be half-hearted about their work. The photo doesn't have to be taken by an expensive photographer, but a photo taken properly not only presents the applicant in the best possible light, it indicates the applicant's sincerity. By going to the trouble of getting a good photo taken, they are saying that they are taking the application itself seriously.

Although we cannot find out everything from a single photo, the face in the photo speaks louder than words. Look closely at the applicant's eyes: the energy will indicate whether they have passion for their work. It may be possible to fake this energy, but the absence of it is a troubling sign.

The expression in the photo is also very important. **Those wearing a gloomy face lack ambition and are unlikely to fit in to the company.** Teamwork is essential in a workplace. If uncertainty is found in the photo, question the applicant about teamwork during the interview.

Work is never a solitary activity. It is heavily influenced by the help of others and human relationships. If any doubts arise from looking at the photo, do not overlook them. Ask a related question in the interview.

Things to look out for:

- Are the eyes in the photo bright and eager? This could indicate keenness to join your company. Dull eyes indicate indifference or a lack of awareness about the importance of creating a good first impression

- Is the photo of poor quality? This could indicate indifference to making a good impression or potential problems in human relationships

2 Points in the entry sheet you should verify (fresh grads)

Fresh grads are mostly inexperienced. They are still comparing work fields and work types. If they filled in an entry sheet at the recruitment test phase, see if they did enough research on the work field and the company.

You can't expect much working experience when recruiting fresh graduates. Focus instead on what they have learnt in the past, their extracurricular activities, their part-time job experiences, and what they have to say about themselves (i.e. their self-evaluations). You are bound to find traces there of their working skills, willingness to work, and stress tolerance. Don't just rely on their reasons for applying and their self-evaluations. During the interview, ask for some episodes of failure and check those too. See if they give you actual episodes or abstract ideas.

If they seem to be considering other fields of work in the recruitment test phase, they are likely to turn down an offer at a later stage or fail to take root in your company. If your company is not the applicant's first priority at the stage of information sessions and recruitment tests, you should definitely think twice before deciding to hire the applicant.

Schools these days teach their students how to fill in an entry sheet and there are manuals explaining the process. Therefore, don't be afraid to ask for more than what is written. It is important to see who the applicant really is.

Checkpoints for the entry sheet

Checkpoints	
Intentions of entry not meant for your company.	
Emphasizing only their school life.	
Giving a vague self-evaluation.	
No comments from a third party.	
Emphasizing only part-time job experiences.	
Drawing no relationship between studies and the work on offer.	
No intention of working on their weaknesses.	
No career plan mentioned.	
Lack of writing ability.	
Have few friends.	

X would be a potentially problematic factor you need to consider

	Suitability and ability	Desire to enter the company	Stress tolerance	Stability
	X	X		X
	X	X		X
	X	X		X
	X		X	X
	X			X
	X	X		
			X	X
		X		X
	X	X		
			X	X

61

(1) Intentions of entry that are not meant for your company

The entry-intention column should indicate that the applicant has understood the content of the information sessions. If the entry intentions are only based on your homepage, your company is not likely to be the applicant's first choice. You need applicants who provide episodes of their studies and part-time work experiences that link up to their intentions of entry. You also need to match the applicants' wannabes to the type of person you need. If they are not sure of what they want to do at the stage of application, they may end up rejecting the job at a later stage.

If your company has a shop front, check if the applicant has been to the shop from their intentions of entry.

Do not just focus on the applicant's wannabes. Make sure they also write about their understanding of what is expected of them.

A good point to check is their passion towards the work field and job type, and their reason for choosing your company over others. Check if they have those stated clearly.

If you have doubts about their intentions of entry after reading their entry sheet, question them on their reasons for applying to your company. If they give vague answers on your company's uniqueness and strengths, you should think twice about hiring them.

Things to look out for:

- Will the applicant reject the offer later if your company is not their first choice?
- Does the applicant appear to have other things they want to do instead of finding a job?

(2) A vague self-evaluation

Information sessions are usually conducted during the recruitment of fresh graduates. It is thus easy to picture the type of person wanted in the industry. **Therefore, if applicants give a vague self-evaluation and fail to tie it up to your company, there may be doubts about their willingness to work, suitability and working ability.**

Some applicants show their understanding of what they would be expected to do in the company, despite their lack of working experience. Those who do so are trying to show their willingness to put to the test what they have learnt in part-time work. If they give you abstract ideas, it means they are unable to self-evaluate. Those applicants may end up quitting the job later, rationalizing that there are jobs more suitable for them out there. Those who list everything in their self-evaluations may be poor communicators. Their conclusions may be all over the place, leaving the reader lost about what they intended to say. Try to focus on the flow of the self-evaluation as well as the content.

Confront those who fail to give examples in an interview of points they have made in their self-evaluation. Applicants who know their own strengths well should be able to apply them to potential work tasks.

Things to look out for:

- Is the applicant unable to self-evaluate?
- Is the applicant uncertain about their wannabes?

(3) Emphasizing only their part-time job experiences

When you only see the records of the applicant's campus activities, part-time job experiences and extracurricular activities, you'd better ask about their academic results during an interview. Although part-time work experience and extracurricular activities serve as a plus on résumés, **it is problematic if applicants provide no information about their formal studies.**

During the interview, question them about the working

periods of their part-time work. If they stress experience of no longer than a few weeks, they are just scraping the bowl for bits and pieces to show you. You can expect those who have been doing the same part-time job for a long time—working no differently than a full-time worker—to have high working ability. However, those applicants sometimes lack humility and eagerness to learn, which are the two characteristics usually found in new recruits.

For those who stress their part-time work experience and extracurricular activities, ask about their vision for the future. There are applicants who have been dreamers throughout their time at university and want to continue that way after graduation. Knuckling down to job-hunting is not the next step for them. Such applicants need to make up their mind and show the right attitude.

Things to look out for:

- Has the applicant ignored their academic record?
- Are the applicant's dreams not about this job?

(4) Lack of background research on the company

Check if what is written matches with the ideal candidate your company is after. Even if the résumé is beautifully written, if the skills and experience recorded have no relevance to your company's requirements, it is likely that your company is not the applicant's first choice. It also shows that the applicant has failed to research the background of your company.

During an interview, you can determine an applicant's level of commitment not only by their answers but also by their attitude and expression. The same goes with entry sheets. **Those who record skills that are likely to be useful to your company, instead of giving vague expressions, are more likely to have a high level of commitment.**

When you find quotes directly extracted from the company overview or recruitment ad, the application is likely to be submitted with an ad hoc purpose. An entry sheet should be written with the required skills and ideal candidate in mind and backed up with experience or qualifications. Those that are not written that way are simply entry sheets for any company in the field. Candidates who have done thorough background research would know not only the glamour of the job, but also the difficulties and challenges that may wait ahead. Check out the applicants' self-evaluation and intentions of entry. See if they are based on solid research and see if the applicants have a clear image of themselves working for your company.

Things to look out for:

- Is your company being treated as just one of many companies in the field?
- Is there a lack of interest and willingness to work?

(5) Strong assumptions

Applicants who make strong assumptions may be misunderstanding the reality. Such people tend to quit when they find that the job differs from what they thought it would be. An interview is required to determine if the applicant has a realistic understanding of the company besides passion. **Those who make strong assumptions are unlikely to befriend their colleagues and supervisors, thus will fail to demonstrate what they have to the full.** Those who have passion towards their job are the ones you should keep an eye out for. However, if their passion is based on personal beliefs, it is likely they will not fit in.

During the interview, check if applicants have not only the passion for, but also the correct understanding of, what they are required to do. Be prepared to explain the reality to those applicants who have made assumptions about your company.

Applicants who apply for jobs based on their assumptions and prejudices tend to regret not doing thorough research after they join the company.

While it is true that you can expect much more from the dreamers than those who lack passion, it is nonetheless essential to have all applicants understand the reality of working for your company before they accept an offer.

Things to look out for:

- Is the applicant likely to quit the job after realizing that reality differs from their dreams?
- Has the applicant conducted any background research on other fields and companies?

(6) Nothing about what they aim to be

Entry sheets with content that is made up just to pass the test may be well written, but there is nothing worthwhile in it. From what is written, you can see if an applicant has applied for the job with an understanding of what they aim to be. Even though the passage may not be perfect, they clearly point out their specific goals and explain how they can fulfill them through working in your company.

It is essential for graduate recruitments that the applicants have work potential. **Those who are low in potential only see what is in front of them, lacking the ability to imagine the near future.** Those who know what they want to do will reach for their goal step by step; however, those who see a job as just any job will fail to clear the first hurdle.

During the interview, ask the applicant about their specific aims. From their response you can tell if they meant what they wrote on their entry sheet. Make sure you check not only their experience and qualifications, but also their future goals, as written on the entry sheet.

Things to look out for:

- Does the applicant know what they want?
- Is the applicant treating your company as just another company?

I will now talk about the points you should focus on while reading a CV and bear in mind during the interviews.

3 Points in the CV you should verify (mid-career)

Job experience strongly influences the recruitment results for mid-career applicants. Thus it is important to determine whether the applicant's job experience is relevant and would come in handy in your company. Even if the applicants are pleasant, if they fail to become suitable workers in a short timeframe, the decision to hire them will be called into question.

Curricula vitae differ from résumés. There is no specific template for writing a CV. Therefore, applicants tend to write only what they want to. Some may even include false experiences on their CV.

If the job experiences written on the CV focus on those related to the recruitment requirements, the applicant will gain credit to a certain extent. Of course, further questioning during the interview will be necessary. Applicants tend to match up their experience with the requirements, in hope of a job. Therefore, it is important not to accept whatever you're given without scrutiny. You must question further during the interview.

To determine the credibility of the CV, it is essential to understand the applicant's intentions. Ask for specific details of their experiences during the interview. Again, accepting everything without questioning may result in a wrong understanding of the applicant's working ability.

Checkpoints for the curriculum vitae

Checkpoints	
Only meets minimal requirements.	
Frequent changes of job in different fields.	
Experience irrelevant to the job.	
More than 4 pages long.	
Nothing about achievements.	
Vague expressions.	
Resigned from former jobs owing to lack of achievement.	
No experience in the advertised field and no linkage with former jobs.	
Intentions vague.	
No emphasis on what is required.	
Typos.	
Experience from several companies bundled as one.	
Handwritten.	
No management experience (when the applicant is over 30).	
Multiple negative expressions.	
Has worked in the former workplace for over ten years.	

X would be a potentially problematic factor that you need to consider.

	Working ability	Desire to enter the company	Willingness to work	Stability
	X	X	X	
	X		X	X
	X	X		X
		X		X
	X			
	X	X		
	X	X		X
	X	X		X
	X	X		X
	X	X		
	X			
	X			X
	X	X	X	
	X			X
			X	X
				X

(1) Only meets minimal requirements

There is not much we can say about applicants' willingness to work and working ability when looking at their CV with only minimal information of the name and job title of their former employment recorded. When the records are not relevant to your company's needs, your company may not be the applicant's first choice. With only minimal information, it is doubtful that we can expect anything from the applicant even if they end up hired.

Some of those who apply while being employed may end up not joining your company even if they receive an unofficial offer. Those applicants' CVs lack passion, thus you should think twice before deciding to hire them.

Applicants who record only minimal information are passive and lack ability to strive higher in work. They also lack presentation skills, thus they may end up having trouble with existing staff. It is also important to double-check whether the applicant has nothing to draw you in, or if they are simply failing to emphasize the right material.

Those who really want to enter your company would find something to say related to the recruitment requirements, even if they only have limited resources.

Things to look out for:

- Has the applicant nothing to draw your interest?
- Does the applicant have a strong will to change jobs or careers?

(2) Lacks a consistent job history

Those who have been leaping between careers may lack consistency and be likely to repeat their own history. **If they are aware of their inconsistency and claim that the future will be different, their credibility should be examined during the interview.** A certain amount of credit should be given to those who try to squeeze out some consistency from an inconsistent history.

You should not dismiss an applicant from consideration because they have had many career changes. You should focus on their working ability and whether it would benefit your company. You should also look at their attitude towards their future career.

Nonetheless, it is true that some applicants who experience quite a few career changes overestimate their abilities. They feel as if no company is seeing them with the right eyes; therefore, they change careers over and over again. There are also some who change careers repeatedly because they cannot connect with their co-workers.

Make sure you check on their reasons for leaving prior employment, and determine if history would repeat itself in your company.

Things to look out for:

- -

- Is the applicant continuously in search of their dream company? They will leave as soon as something better appears
- Has the applicant a low tolerance for stress? They will leave as soon as something unpleasant occurs

(3) Document too long

There is no fixed template for a CV. **Those who write long essays without paragraphing and spacing their words may have loads of passion, but they lack the ability to think in the reader's shoes.** Those who think about the reader would add subheadings to their passage and write no more than 300 characters in Japanese per topic.

Those who are unable to express what they have in mind are likely to lack the ability to prioritize, thus ending up failing to increase their sales even though they work hard. This type of applicant usually neglects others' feelings and babbles on and on during a group interview.

There is no word limit for a CV. However, it should

be no more than three pages long. Some applicants in the technology field tend to list all the projects they have been involved in, resulting in lengthy CVs of more than five pages. However, if the listed projects are not of interest to the company, no one will want to read about them. It is not necessary to sieve out all the applicants who hand in lengthy CVs, nor is the length of the CV an indicator of the applicants' passion. But bear in mind to check out their working attitude and personality at the interview stage.

Things to look out for:

- Does the applicant have a tendency to make strong assumptions, causing them to neglect their true surroundings?
- Has the applicant listed everything they have ever done regardless of its relevance in the misapprehension that it will make a good impression?

(4) Not emphasizing job experiences that would benefit the company

A CV is a piece of presentation material that explains what the applicant has done that is relevant to the recruiting company. However, when experiences that would stand out for your company are not emphasized, the chances are that the applicant is handing out the same CV to every other company. If your company is the first on the applicant's list, the applicant would be likely to give an impression that they have done thorough background research. Otherwise, your company may be no more than just another company to the applicant.

Even if the job is in field where the applicant lacks experience, those who are keen will squeeze out some relevance from their history. **CVs that stress nothing belong to applicants who recycle their CV without tailoring it to suit the particular job.** Such applicants have a high chance of ending up as people who only do what they are told and lack the ability to work constructively, even if they do enter the company. Thus you should think twice before making a favorable decision.

Even with a glamorous profile, applicants that lack understanding of what they are expected to do in the recruiting company will be low in motivation at work, and nothing much can be expected of them.

Things to look out for:

- Does the applicant have no idea about the expectations of the recruiting company?
- Does the applicant appear passive and lack a positive attitude to work?

(5) Experience of over ten years in a former workplace

There are recruitment personnel that give a high mark to those applicants who have worked for more than ten years in their former workplace and have experienced little career change. However, some of those applicants may be attached to their former workplace and fail to adapt to a new environment. If their job experience is what you are looking for, the reality about your company should be explained thoroughly to the applicant and their understanding gained before you decide to hire them.

Given the long period the applicant has worked in their former workplace, **it may be hard for them to adapt to a new way of working in a new company. Some people also fail in constructing relationships with existing staff, resulting in them changing careers repeatedly.** While those who have a long history of working in the same company may have higher credit than those who change their jobs often, the decision should nonetheless be made depending on what they are able to do for the company's benefit and their vision for the future.

Arguably, those applicants who have experienced what it is like to change jobs regularly will have a higher adaptability to a new environment. They are also less likely to expect too much. On the other hand, some of those who are changing jobs for the first time may expect to be trained and taught from scratch, just like a fresh grad. Even though they may have changed jobs because of poor business performance, don't rule them out: it may be that they are ready to start again with a brand new self.

Things to look out for:

- Is the applicant likely to make comparisons with their old job and not be content?
- Will the applicant fail to integrate into the new environment?

(6) Bundling up experience from various employment agencies

While your focus should be on the performance and working ability of the applicant rather than their former type of employment, it is still worthwhile to grasp how long the applicant was employed in all their previous jobs. This is difficult to do when applicants simply record their registration period in several employment agencies and fail to present their exact working periods. Try figuring them out through an interview.

The applicant may have registered in an employment agency for five years and been allocated to three companies to work casually during that period. However, the exact period the applicant has been working may be less than two years. There could be problems with such applicants after recruitment.

There are good quality workers that do not have full-time working experience. However, when deciding to hire such applicants as full-time staff, you will need to be careful about the working conditions you offer.

Some casual workers intend to change to full-time work in the hope of acquiring a more stable income. **Their hopes in this respect are their own business. Unless they fulfill the skills or experience required, and have a strong determination to work for your company, they should have little chance of being hired full-time.** Do not just focus on their working ability during an interview. Check out their working attitude, determination, and career vision as well.

Things to look out for:

- Are the applicant's stated working experiences deceiving?
- Does the applicant lack the working ability required?

Column 2

Point out the applicant's mistakes

During an episode where I was preforming a mock interview with a job hunter, she spread her application documents out on the table and started reading aloud from her CV. Usually, we put nothing on the table during an interview, but for some reason this job hunter had always spread out her information on the table during every interview. I asked her if the interviewers had ever said anything to her about it. They had not, and she constantly failed to get a job offer. I wonder why the interviewers did not just tell her to put away her documents.

Don't be afraid of destroying the relationship you are building with the applicant by pointing out their mistakes. It is better for them if you do point them out. This job hunter was unsuccessful not because there was any problem with her qualifications, but because she did not know interview etiquette. (Later on, she did find herself a job.)

Also, bear in mind that if you decide to not give an offer due to a bad first impression, you may be missing out on people who could be of benefit to your company.

CHAPTER 3

KNOW THE BASICS
OF INTERVIEWING

Interviewing is the most important recruitment test. During an interview, you need to see through to the core of the applicant to decide if they are the one for your company—and you need to do it quickly.

1 Guidance for interviewers

While it is difficult for one person to judge another, the interviewer must be able to pull out what is hidden in the paperwork and written tests. Interviewers are not question-generators. The job of an interviewer is twofold: to trigger the applicant into giving a truthful answer and to decide whether to hire the applicant or not. To do so, the interview should be constructed in an environment where the applicant can talk in comfort. If the interview is conducted with stilted questions, all you will get will be stilted answers.

Your decision to hire can be made after the interview. During the interview, you need to focus on digging into the positives of the interviewee's personality and experience. If you simply lose interest because of a bad first impression, the applicant will never open up to you. Even if you are not impressed with their academic record or job history, don't let it show on your face or in your attitude.

You must never deny the applicant's experience or way of thinking. Try to understand them. This applies to more than just interviews. Trust is built on the basis of understanding.

If you could decide whether to hire a person simply by reading through their paperwork, there would be no need to go through an interview. In interviews, you dig deeper into what is written on the paper, checking its veracity. You also dig into what is not written in black and white, and discover the personality of the applicant. To achieve these goals, the interviewer must give the applicant the impression that they understand what they are saying.

Some interviewers mistakenly treat an interview as a counseling session. Those interviewers are very eager to share their thoughts and opinions and offer advice. However, the interviewer's words are not part of the material used to determine an applicant's results. Try hard to listen to the applicants and create a comfortable environment for them to present themselves.

From the answers they provide, determine whether the applicant has the skills, ability, and passion that your company is after. Ask yourself whether they are "the one" for your company.

And don't forget—at the same time as you are judging the interviewee, they are judging you and the company you represent.

Constructing a relationship of trust during a short

interview is key to recruiting good-quality staff.

Tips for being a good interviewer:

- Be sincere
- Don't not let first impressions affect you one way or the other
- Provide an environment for the applicant to speak in comfort
- Construct a relationship of trust by listening to the applicant and showing understanding
- Be conscious of you bear for future of the company and applicant

2 Three features to focus on

There are three features you should focus on in an interview: the applicant's character, the applicant's ability, and the applicant's self-evaluation.

(1) The applicant's character

Even if the applicant has high working ability, they won't stay and bring benefit to the company if they don't fit in. For example, if the applicant appears passive, as though their heart is not in their application, there is not much point in hiring them. However, even if they leave a bad impression after an interview, you should see if it is something that can be fixed.

An applicant's communication ability can be observed through an interview. **Keep your eyes on their ability to understand and react to the interviewer's questions correctly.** If the applicant fails to listen and has strong opinions, they may end up only doing the jobs that they are interested in.

Everyone tries to present themselves at their best during an interview. To get beyond the facade, conduct a pressure test (see also Chapter 6). It will help reveal the applicant's tolerance to stress. If the applicant has changed jobs frequently within a short period, challenge them about this. They might have good reasons (or fixable reasons) or they might have a weak-willed character and be the sort of person who loses interest in things easily.

Tips for judging the applicant's character:

- Judge the applicant's strengths and weaknesses through their self-evaluation and interview presentation
- Check out their attitude and preparation
- Conduct a pressure test
- Conduct an aptitude test

(2) The applicant's ability

Fresh graduates, of course, lack work experience. Their working ability can be assessed through their studies, part-time work experience, SPI (synthetic personality inventory), and other written tests. For mid-career applicants, their job history serves as information to determine whether they are suitable for your company.

Those who understand their strengths from their job history and are able to present their strengths in front of an interviewer are promising applicants. **When vague answers are given, you should check the applicant**

once more by conducting a written exam to test their working ability. You can't expect much from applicants who brag about their past. The main factors to consider during recruitment should be the applicant's understanding of the job and if they present themselves as a potential asset to the company.

Tips for judging the applicant's ability:

- For new graduates, check out the applicant's major subjects (and any part-time or volunteer experience)
- For mid-career recruits, check out their workplace strengths

(3) The applicant's self-evaluation

Check why the applicant applied to your company over others, as stated in their self-evaluation. You can't hope for much motivation from those who apply to just any company. **The applicant's willingness to work, passion, and reasons for applying to your particular company should all be assessed for their credibility.** You need to use the interview to determine whether the applicant really meant what they said in their self-evaluation and their written reasons for wanting to join your company.

Tips for assessing the applicant's self-evaluation:

- Check out their intentions of entry and self-evaluation
- Look closely at the way they listen, the way they speak, their expressions, and their overall attitude

3 Understand the applicant's point of view

The right staff will work with flying colors in your company, so the company should create an environment that more people will want to work in. There are no companies who get the staff they want by doing nothing to understand the applicant's point of view.

At the application stage, most applicants are thinking about things like improving their careers, possible problems with the working environment, the working conditions, and other points centered on their own personal wellbeing. Most applicants don't think about contributing and bringing merit to the company at this stage.

While no company can fulfill all applicants' desires 100 percent, it is wise to try your best to understand what your applicants are looking for and fulfill their wishes as much as you are able. At the same time, it is wise to have a close look during an interview to see if the applicant is thinking at all about how they can bring benefits to your company. Because applicants' points of view can differ from that of the company (and even from each other), the applicants with the largest area of agreement with the company are the ones to look out for.

Once the applicant's prioritized wishes are fulfilled, the trust relationship constructed between interviewer and interviewee becomes crucial to the applicant's decision to join the company.

Thinking from the applicant's point of view, preparing a good working environment for them and ensuring there is a career path are factors that will greatly affect the success of your recruiting efforts.

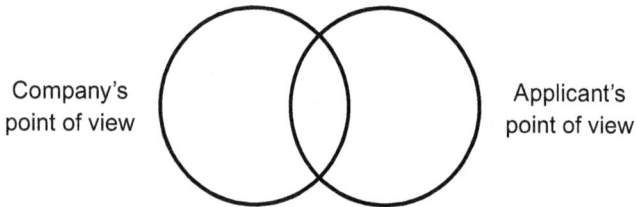

Company's point of view

Applicant's point of view

The larger the area of agreement between the two, the better the match.

What the applicant is thinking:

- Is this the place where I can fulfill my dreams?
- Is this an environment where I can improve my career?
- Do the working conditions of this job match my expectations?
- Will I have a senior mentor to look after me?

- Is this a stable job?
- Did I receive a good impression of the company as a whole from the interviewer?

What the interviewer is thinking:

- Do they have the required skill and experience? Are they fit for the job?
- Do they understand their own strengths?
- Do they have the passion to join this company?
- Do they have the ability to accommodate to a group?
- Are they able to self-evaluate?
- Do the labor conditions match their hopes?

4 Do not conduct an interview with a condescending attitude

An interview is conducted to find out if an applicant is suitable. However, if the interview is conducted with a condescending attitude, the applicant will not receive a good impression, leading to failure to recruit good staff.

An interviewer with a condescending attitude is one who wears arrogance on their face and speaks with a haughty tone. They look down on applicants, thinking that they have a higher status over them because the interviewers are the ones who make the offers. These types of interviewers also tend to base their final decision to hire on their own personal preferences.

If you believe that it is the company who decides to hire the applicant, you are overlooking the fact that the applicant can decline your offer. If you conduct the interview with a highhanded attitude, the applicant will feel uncomfortable and refuse to open up to you. It is very important to construct a good relationship with the interviewee during the short timeframe of an interview, as the applicants will then see your company as one that they would like to work for.

At the application stage, most applicants only see your company as just one company they are interested in. During the recruitment process, they may then gain more interest in your company and list it as their first preference. This is also one of the goals of interviewing.

An interview conducted with a condescending attitude will only leave the applicant uninterested and you will only be able to scratch the surface of the applicant's potential. An arrogant attitude will not result in the applicant wanting to know more about your company. During the interview, try to imagine the applicant as one that will chose your company over other companies.

Interviewers need to be aware that applicants use interviewers' words, tone, and presentation to help them decide whether the company is worth spending a significant part of their life in. The interviewer is the bridge between the company and the applicant.

For service industries, the applicants you turn down may become your customers someday, and it is never wise to show arrogance to a potential customer.

It is said that the interviewee's attitude reflects that of the interviewer. When an interview is conducted with a highhanded attitude, the applicant decides that this company is not worth it and responds in kind. They may look calm and pleasant, but they may not be so inside.

Interviewers who receive many declines to the offers they make should re-examine their interview techniques. Their attitude would definitely change if they could come to see applicants as valued "future customers."

Signs of an interviewer having a condescending attitude:

- Does not smile
- Holds their own thoughts strongly and refuses to compromise with applicants
- Refuses to listen to what they are not interested in
- Makes their decisions based only on academic and job histories
- Bases their questions only on set questions related to an applicant's self-evaluation
- Fails to dig deeper into the applicant's answers
- Conducts interviews under high pressure
- Does not have ambition to the interview
- Does not thank the applicant
- Shows their arrogance in their facial expression, tone of voice, and body language

5 Qualities of a good interviewer

The qualities of a good interviewer are many and varied.

Applicants come hoping for a job, and so they have a tendency to give elaborate and exaggerated answers, hiding their negative attributes. In the short timeframe of an interview, interviewers need to see through all that, meaning they have to be careful not to be carried away by the applicant's self-evaluation in order to decide if they are truly suited to the company.

Being interested in human behavior and growth is one of the signs of a good interviewer. If the interviewer has no interest in people, a simply practical interview could be conducted, followed by making a uniform decision. **A person's possibilities are endless, but if the interviewer is not interested in people, it will be impossible for them to discover the applicant's strengths.**

Instead of using deduction, those who like people tend to score others by adding up their attributes, in the hope of discovering their positives.

When an interviewer feels doubt about an applicant, the applicant will be sure to pick up on this feeling. Such applicants will fail to form a good impression at the interview and will tend to give noncommittal answers, making it hard to determine their true nature. On the other hand, applicants who form a good impression of the interviewer tend to relax and speak their heart out.

On the other hand, an interview is no place to enjoy a conversation. Interviewers who enjoy the interview may build a connection with the interviewee, but they will struggle when needing to decide if the applicant should become a member of the workforce. When points of doubt are found in the applicant, it is essential to ask the hard questions. When interviewers fail to ask the hard questions for fear of destroying the warm atmosphere created, the chances of making a mismatch will be high.

Interviewers also need to be experts in the company's operation and HR organization strategy. Applicants who feel that the interviewer is inexperienced and knows little about their own company tend to look down on the interviewer. However, inexperienced interviewers who are sincere and try to give an answer to the applicant's questions are highly rated by applicants, despite their inexperience. Applicants who receive a good impression will tend to be positive about your company's future. So try to construct an interview that will bring out the passion in the applicants and lead them to want to join your company.

Good interviewers:

- are interested in human behavior and growth
- are considerate
- give a good impression and seem trustworthy
- do not make emotive decisions
- know the company well
- are caring and warm
- present well when answering the applicant's questions
- are good at discovering the positives in people

6 Traps interviewers fall into easily

By understanding the traps interviewers tend to fall into, we can determine if the interviewer has made the right decision. People construct and conduct interviews, thus there will be differences in personality and ways of thought. However, through understanding the potential traps, mistakes in decision-making can be prevented.

[Halo effect]

When the applicant has a good academic background or a good job history, everything about them tends to be highly rated. It is true that an applicant's potential as a good worker is enhanced by the quality of the university they attended or the reputation of the companies they have worked for. However, a wrong decision may be made unless you look closely at what they have learned through their experiences and what they can do for your company. One outstanding factor does not mean the applicant is perfect, and the reverse is also true: one problematic factor does not mean the applicant is no good.

[Central tendency]

"Central tendency" refers to the tendency not to mark the

applicant as good or bad, but as neither good nor bad, which is not very helpful when it comes to making a final decision. While the final decision is usually left to the final interview, earlier interviewers should nonetheless try to record helpful remarks instead of just sending the applicant through to the next stage with non-committal remarks.

[Contrast error range]

"Contrast error range" refers to a tendency for interviewers to assign remarks to an applicant based on the applicant who has just left, instead of objectively. This means the better the prior applicant, the more likely the current applicant will be underestimated, and vice versa. As the interviewer is using their personal feelings, applicants tend to be either underestimated or overestimated.

[Tendency to be too lenient]

There is a tendency to rate the applicant too leniently when the interviewer has enjoyed the chitchat in the interview. You may receive complaints from the applicant's allocated department that the applicant is a charming person but not a good worker. Although chitchat is necessary to sooth tension during an interview, it should not preclude you from taking a hard look at the applicant's working ability as well, even if the interview has been an enjoyable experience.

[Tendency to overrate passion]

Although it is important for an applicant to show passion towards your company, a passionate applicant may also be harboring illusions and will resign when they find out that the reality is different from their dreams. To prevent this, avoid rating a person only for their passion and willingness to work, and make sure they understand the reality of working for your company.

7 Training tips for a likable interviewer

Interviewers tend to rate a person from the applicant's attitude, expressions, and clothing, as well as their abilities. The applicant rates the company by the interviewer. Therefore, it is important for the interviewer to be likable.

Mock interviews are a good way of increasing the likability of the interviewer. Through mock interviews, you can assess if applicants would be inspired to join the company after meeting the interviewer.

Nonverbal communication such as facial expressions and attitudes speak louder than words. Salespeople are always careful how they present themselves because they want to give a good impression to their clients. Interviewers should also try to give a good impression to applicants during an interview.

Record the mock interview and check the recordings with other interviewers. Interviewers can also check on their tone and way of speech through recording voice messages. Applicants may not unleash complaints on the interviewer for their arrogant attitude, but no one will want to join the company after such an experience. **Applicants will not want to spend time in such a company unless they can see interest and care in how the interviewer looks at them.** As the interviewer is usually not thinking of themselves as an object of judgment, they may lack awareness of how they are presenting themselves.

The status of the interviewer can also affect the recruitment process. It is hard to recruit applicants whose status is higher than that of the interviewer. To recruit a good workforce, interviewers should be someone that an applicant would be happy to work for.

A likable interviewer:

- dresses well
- thanks the applicant for applying and makes eye contact
- thanks the applicant for coming to the interview
- does not give an impression that the interview is being conducted in between other jobs
- keeps smiling while speaking
- speaks slowly and clearly
- keeps their tone of voice happy and lively
- sits straight and listens calmly
- responds when the applicant speaks
- does not deny anything the applicant says
- looks closely at all the applicants in a group interview

- does not ask much about the applicant's private life
- responds to the applicant's questions

8 How to construct an interview

An interview has a basic flow. The first five to ten minutes are usually taken up in explaining the job workload, asking questions about the applicant's self-evaluation and establishing the applicant's intentions should an offer be made. This is the first stage of the interviewer determining whether to recruit the applicant. The next ten minutes will be spent digging deeper to see if the applicant's performance matches the impression they have just given. The last five minutes is given over to the applicants' questions and to providing them with an opportunity to demonstrate how keen they are to get the job.

Keenness is important because those whom you want to recruit may decline your offer or resign from the job if they do not have a strong will to work for your company. During the second half of the interview, determine if they would be likely to enter the company if given an offer.

The first ten minutes after the applicant enters the room is the time you get to know the most about the applicant. However, if you make your decision during the first half of the interview, you may slacken off during the second half.

Even though the applicant may not appear to be what you are looking for, try nonetheless to dig out some gold.

If you find the perfect applicant, don't try to persuade them to join the company during the last five minutes of the interview. A CEO friend of mine once asked the applicants during a fresh graduate recruitment to tell him how likely it was that they would join the company if an offer was made. He told me that he would not hire anyone who gave anything less than 100 percent as their answer. However, most of his successful applicants ended up resigning from the company. If you force the applicants to show their eagerness to enter the company, they will end up feeling awkward. The second half of the interview should be used instead to build up a trust relationship with the applicant. Determine the applicant's eagerness through their speech, facial expression, and how they present themselves.

Interview lengths will vary depending on the particular company and type of work. But, as a guide, **an interview should end within 40 minutes. A long interview would sap concentration and be of no help in determining the true self of the applicant.** A short interview might make applicants think that the company has not seen enough of them, making them think twice about accepting an offer.

Do not just construct an interview; understand the flow of a good interview.

The flow of a good interview

[The start]

In the first ten minutes of the interview you should get through the basics of introductions, questions about intentions, reasons for leaving their former job, and self-evaluation. Look closely at the applicant's personality and ask questions to dig deeper. Explain the particular position on offer and make a mental note if the applicant could be someone you are looking for.

[The middle]

Dig deeper still. Ask questions based on the answers to the basic questions asked in the first ten minutes. Make sure the applicant understands the working conditions, and verify the impression you formed of the applicant during the first ten minutes.

[The last part]

Answer the applicant's questions. Look for passion and willingness in the applicant. Make the final decision.

9 Constructing a trust relationship with the applicant

To see the true self of the applicant, it is important to build up a trust relationship during the interview. This boils down to saying what you mean and meaning what you say. There are interviewers who say, "There is no true personality: all the answers are prepared and rehearsed", or "An interview is too short to develop a trust relationship." It is true that applicants tend to present themselves so as to impress the interviewers. **However, by probing beyond the basics and creating an environment in which an applicant can speak freely, it is possible to see the true self of the applicant.** To do so, soften the "choosing" atmosphere and create a relaxing environment for the applicants to answer the interviewer's questions. A relaxed environment cannot be created if the interviewer has a stern face and plainly asks all the questions the applicant expects. A relaxed environment is not a back-at-home environment, but it should be an environment in which the applicant feels they can speak out.

Being empathic and building trust with their clients is important for a counselor, and the same can be said about an interviewer. Applicants do not only judge the interviewer by their words, but by observing their facial expressions and attitudes. Therefore, a gloomy face does not help in building a trust relationship.

Nod when the applicant makes a point, and do not deny anything they say. Throw in appropriate words after the applicant speaks. By giving such agreeable responses, the applicant feels that the interviewer is trying to understand, thus being someone the applicant can open up to. Simply reading the interview requirement sheet without giving the applicant a response enforces the "checking factor" and does not bring out the applicant's true personality.

As well as throwing in agreeable responses, repeating part of the applicant's words can help break the ice. To dig into the applicant's inner self, interviewers need to be aware that they should leave it to the applicants to speak, instead of speaking too much themselves.

The final recruitment decision can be made after seeing the true self of the applicant (that is, after the interview), so during the interview just focus on pulling out strands of information to refer to later.

Actions that show empathy:

- Giving agreeable responses

- Looking interested
- Repeating part of what the applicant says
- Listening to their responses and giving positive comments

Ways to build a trust relationship with the applicant:

- Show empathy
- Make eye contact when speaking
- Look very interested when listening to their answers
- Throw in appropriate words after each phrase
- Dig deeper, based on the answers received

10 Find the applicant through two-way communication

Do not just listen to the applicant's words—seem interested and create an environment for two-way communication.

Add credibility to the applicant's response by questioning further, based on their response. By creating two-way communication, the applicant is able to speak with their own words, thus giving the interviewer a glimpse of their true self.

Imagine a daily conversation. If you just give blunt responses such as "yes" or "maybe" while listening to someone speaking, they will think that you are not interested, and quickly end the conversation. If you are silent or monosyllabic while listening to the applicant speaking, the interview will be nothing but a useless ceremony.

A ceremonial interview tells you no more than the documents have already told you. The aim of an interview is to dig deeper into the credibility of what the documents say, and discover factors about the applicant that are not printed on the sheets of paper.

An environment with communication going both ways is evidence that the interviewer is interested in the applicant's responses. When the interviewer is interested, they will think of more questions to ask, thus drawing out spontaneous, unrehearsed responses from the applicant.

Interviewers who simply keep quiet and listen do not give a good impression to the applicants. The applicants feel that it is not worthwhile to go on talking. All the interviewer will hear will be rehearsed and prepared words.

When the applicant gets excited during an interview, it is because the interviewer has showed interest and the applicant was able to speak from the heart.

Two-way communication is not only a tool to dig out information for the final decision, it also makes the applicant feel understood, increasing their eagerness to work for your company.

To establish two-way communication:

- Be interested in the applicant's response

  ↓

- Do not just listen. Ask more questions and dig deeper

  ↓

- Give the applicant the impression that you are interested in them

  ↓

- Draw out the applicant's own words, instead of those prepared and rehearsed

  ↓

- Let them speak from the heart, so that you can glimpse their true personality

  ↓

- Find credibility and personality in their words

11 Apply Maslow's law

Maslow's hierarchy of needs is a motivation theory based on five needs—basic physiological needs (the need to function physically), security (the need to feel safe), social (the need to belong), esteem (the need for respect), and self-actualization (the need for self-fulfillment). People reach self-actualization by successively acquiring these needs, starting from the most basic. Maslow's law says that once a need is satisfied it stops being a motivator.

By determining which stage of the hierarchy the applicant is sitting on, you can get closer to their core personality.

Good workers aim at self-actualization through building their own careers. However, different people are needed for different companies for different positions, thus mismatches can occur. Through failing to determine which stage of the hierarchy the applicant stands on, they may end up not being suitable to the type of work in your company and fail to stay.

Interviewers should try to understand the type of person needed for the position during recruitment instead of just picking the best one out of the pack. For example, those who aim at self-actualization would get fed up with simple day-to-day work. Those who have strong self-esteem might want to work individually, and might leave the company after learning all the know-hows. In order to prevent mismatching, look closely at the applicant's aims and their way of working, thus matching the right applicant to the right job.

maslow's hierarchy
of needs

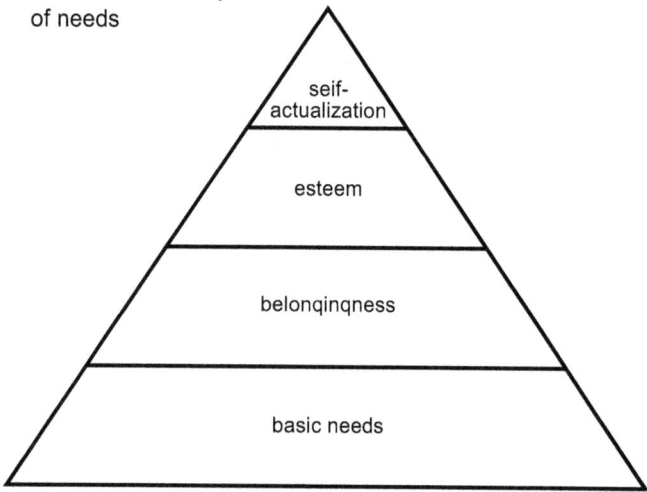

seif-
actualization

esteem

belonqinqness

basic needs

[Self-actualization]

People at the top-level of the hierarchy desire self-fulfillment through their work. Their career is their center and they desire to go higher. They tend to work with a strong belief in themselves.

Pros : High achievement can be expected as they are always aiming higher.

Cons : You won't get them to stay unless they find an aim to fulfill.

[Esteem]

This type of person tends to be independent and has a strong will. They are highly capable of responding to challenges and have a very strong desire to improve, thus you can expect sales to grow fast in their hands. They also deal well with setbacks and difficulties.

Pros : Strong self-awareness to improve; capable of dealing with troubles.

Cons : They may not get on well with their manager unless they agree with their workload.

[Belongingness]

They long to befriend their colleagues and work in a friendly environment. They tend to be nice people, but they may not have outstanding working abilities. However, they are willing to take on challenges.

Pros : They blend into the team during teamwork.

Cons : They don't aim high and are not natural leaders.

[Basic needs/security]

Applicants who work for money and security aim for places with a fair pay, and the better the pay the more they like the company. Money is their basic motivator, but applicants may choose companies for their pay and fail to stay.

Pros : Suitable to work in a stable working environment.

Cons : They lack self-improvement awareness and are passive when it comes to work.

Questions that apply to Maslow's law:

What is your motivation for going to work?

If they prioritize the working conditions, they would be on the basic needs level. If their priority is on cooperativeness, they may sit on the belongingness level. From their answers you will be able to define their level.

What do you see as self-fulfillment?

Those who have lots to talk about will have a strong desire for self-actualization.

Have you gained experience from failures?

By listening to how they overcame difficulties and met challenges, we can determine their position on the hierarchy.

12 Check out their EQ

Good workers are people who have a high stress tolerance **and grow with the help of the people around them.** In short, they have high EQ (emotional quotient), also known as "emotional intelligence." An applicant's EQ will show you whether they will become good workers or not.

People who have high EQ not only understand themselves, they also try to understand others through getting help from others. Furthermore, they are able to control their emotions even when they fail, quickly finding their next aim and new challenge. Business is no solo-play for them. Those who achieve high with help from others will be the ones who make great achievements. IQ is an inborn ability, but EQ builds up with experience. Those who do well in school may not be the ones who benefit the company the most. If the final decision is made purely on academic results, mismatching may occur after recruitment.

Those who cooperate with their colleagues to achieve their goals and those who set a new goal after falling down are the ones to look out for. It is important not only to look at their academic results and achievements, but also to look at their résumé, job history, and working style.

People who have high EQ:

- Understand themselves and others
- Can control their emotions and actions
- Have strong will to achieve their goals
- Build good relationships
- Achieve their goals with the help of others
- Make full use of the help and support of others

Questions to check an applicant's EQ:

Please tell me specifically what you have learnt from a past failure.

Those with high EQ will be the ones who are not beaten by their failure, but learn from the experience and apply it to a fresh challenge.

Have you achieved anything as part of a team?

Check out their experience of working as part of a team in club activities, projects, and casual work.

Are you able to control your emotions when things aren't going well?

People who have high EQ are able to control their

emotions and pick themselves up from the ground. Dig deeper for specific ways they control themselves.

How do you accommodate with others?

Those with high EQ can specifically describe how they work with others, proving they know how to accommodate.

13 Interviews for casual and part-time jobs

When interviewing for casual and part-time positions, it is important to check if the applicant matches the working qualities, communication ability, and stress tolerance required. Most applicants apply for casual work for the working conditions, thus it would be too harsh to ask for strong passion for the company. Working conditions and wages would be their priority when given the choice. When you don't seem to get a good crowd, try comparing your conditions with other companies. Although the job itself is a priority when the applicant makes their decision, the working conditions will also be important. In the past, I have recruited for part-time cleaners for beauty salons. We received a large number of applications when we named the position "Beauty Lady." I believe that we would not have received such a number of applications if we had just recruited for a "Cleaner."

The position may be casual or part-time, but such staff would still work as part of the company's workforce and become the face of the company. Therefore the position is not open to just anyone. **During an interview, make sure that they have no problem with the labor conditions, and that they are comfortable with the interview.**

The family's support should also be checked during an interview. Their way of overcoming difficulties should also be questioned, so as to see how they deal with stress. The applicant's motivation will be strongly affected by how you explain the position. So don't just tell the applicants about the workload—tell them more about the achievements of part-time and casual staff, and how rewarding and interesting the job can be.

There are applicants who are unsure if they are capable of the job. Make them feel secure by telling them about your company's training system. Indeed, there are cases of casual and part-time staff making a stronger workforce than full-time workers.

If the interview is sloppy or too casual, because it is not recruitment for full-time staff, the applicants will definitely feel it. Conduct the interview as you would when recruiting for full-time staff, and create an environment for the applicant to relax in.

Sometimes you labor conditions don't match the applicant's requirements, but don't just give up. Try to find a resolution and plan together. Not all applicants will become your staff, but they may become your customers one day. Therefore, make sure you contact them politely about deferring their application.

Points to look out for when recruiting for casual and part-time positions:

- Do their hopes match the requirements?
- Do they have problems at school or at home?
- Do they present themselves well to give a good impression?
- Are they able to cooperate with others?
- Are they able to overcome failures and difficulties?
- Do they understand the workload and are they capable of carrying out the work?

14 See through their lies

Keep in mind that applicants who have been turned down several times may lie about their negative attributes. Interview questions are usually based on the applicant's résumé, entry sheet, and job history or CV. However, while recruiting mid-career, if nobody questions a big blank period on the résumé, it will be impossible to track down jobs that are not listed on their CV. There are career counselors that suggest applicants leave out jobs they have done for only a short period. Of course, it is up to the applicant to include the job or not. However, if they lie about any blank periods, it will mean that their résumé is a fake. Even if the truth comes out after the recruitment, the applicant can still get away with it by saying that they were not asked about it during the interview.

If the applicant says that they have been upgrading themselves during the blank period, ask them what they have done specifically. They may tell lies as they try to fill in the long gap.

If their reason for leaving their prior workplace is because they were fired, dig down further. Some interviewers assume the problem is the company's business problem, and so do not ask questions. However, you may later find out that it was the applicant who was to blame. Once again, they have the excuse that they were not asked during the interview.

Applicants try their best not to give answers that will interfere with their chances of getting the job. **If you start by being doubtful about everything, it will be difficult for the applicant to trust you. So try not to be caught checking everything that you find questionable in their documents.**

Those who tell you that they purposely left out jobs that they have done for only a short time are fine. And it is a good thing to upgrade oneself during a blank period. The main problem is the attitude of the applicant who lies even when they are questioned directly. Those who lie avoid eye contact with the interviewer. When an applicant looks around, speaks softly, and fails to speak clearly, they are likely to be lying. Try to question further to make sure.

Points to check out:

- Long blank periods
- → Check what they have done during the time

- Self-improvement
→ Check if they have skills and abilities that would benefit your company
- Involuntary retirement
→ Ask about their specific reasons
- Giving vague answers on their achievements and performance
→ Ask for details

15 Conduct an aptitude test

An aptitude test may help you see the true self of the applicant more quickly. It can reveal the applicant's working style and stress tolerance, which are hard to determine during an interview. We all have our own behavior pattern. The interviewer should not expect the applicant to think the same way as themselves and judge applicants accordingly. **An aptitude test may show more than the interviewer can find during an interview.**

There are different types of aptitude tests, and none should be taken too literally. Don't let the results bias you during the interview. The results of the test serve only as reference material and should only affect the final decision by around 30 percent. Even if the test results indicate that the applicant should not be hired, you might miss out on a good applicant by slacking off during the interview, thinking that it is a waste of time. The test results should be analyzed to find the reasons for not hiring the applicant. If stress tolerance is the problem, you should check it out during the interview and then make the final decision afterwards. If the test results show that there is a problem with honesty, the applicant is likely to lie at work. Check on their credibility during the interview.

Certain factors may influence the results of an aptitude test, so remember to think twice about the linkage between the recruiting job and the test results. If the test results do not match the job type, the applicant may not become a good worker.

By conducting an aptitude test, and analyzing the results before conducting an interview, you will be better able to see through to the true self of the applicant. Aptitude tests are a good tool for recruitment, and serve as an important document for HR to make the final decision.

Points to glean from an aptitude test:

Listed below are the things you can find out from an aptitude test (with reference to the COMPASS aptitude test).

- Action prediction (active, achievement-oriented, challenge–oriented, consistent, communicative, accommodative, responsible etc.)
- Attention points (tolerant to depression and anxiety, dependent, avoidance behavior, emotional, impulsive, self-centered)
- Style of interpersonal relations
- Tolerance to stress

- Capable
- Job ability
- Sedentary
- Overall remarks

Column 3

A word to relieve the tension

There are applicants who are not able to answer questions because of nerves. Give them a gentle word, such as "Try to relax and make yourself comfortable. I'm a bit nervous, too, to be honest." applicants who are nervous may have a strong eagerness to enter the company, thus they may have stressed themselves over the possibility of not getting the job. If you decide not to hire the applicant simply because they were nervous, you may be missing out. One of the women I conducted a mock interview with was not comfortable with making eye contact with the interviewer, so she always looked down. After many times of training her to look at the interviewer as she spoke, she was able to speak with a confidence she had lacked before. She then got a job offer. One of the aims of an interview is to see the real self of the applicant. Therefore, it is the interviewer's job to relieve the applicant's nerves. Sometimes our emotions mirror those of others. When we feel that the applicant is nervous, we may seem nervous too. Please create an environment comfortable enough for the applicant to answer your questions.

CHAPTER 4

FIND THE TRUTH
BEHIND ACTIONS
AND ATTITUDES

To reach the core of the applicant, you should look beyond their documents and interview responses. Those who have two faces act differently from their normal self during interviews. This may become a problem after they join the company.

1 See form the process of application to visiting the company

[From the initial phone call]

You can catch a glimpse of what the applicant is like through their initial phone call about their application. Those that hang up straight after dispensing with the necessities are self-centered and neglectful of others' feelings. Those that fail to give responses over the phone and can't decide on when to schedule their interview may be indecisive and lack judgment. You can also assess their communication skills by how well they can explain their situation clearly and how well they appear to understand the company. As a rule, phone calls should not be made early in the morning or after work. However, those who lack manners may call at their own convenience.

[From the state of their documents]

When sending in their documents, the applicants who ensure their documents don't get crushed in transit are those who work with care. On the other hand, those who don't attach a support to their documents and leave them bent and folded may lack attention to detail.

[From the arrival time]

Check on their arrival time for the interview. Those who arrive early show keenness to join the company, although those who come more than 30 minutes early during a mid-career recruit may be self-centered and lack consideration for the other party.

Applicants who look around the company may not be considering your company as their first priority. They could be thinking that the company is not for them. Keep an eye on the applicant's attitude and facial expressions at the reception. If they are too relaxed, as if it is not part of the interview, the applicant may turn out to have two faces.

The impression formed by the person on reception, whether good or bad, is important material to factor into your final decision. Try to develop a system in which reception staff can chip in a word or two.

At the application stage:

- Calling in during busy hours
→ Possible problems with their business manners
- Problems when dealing with phone calls
→ Lack of communication skills

- Problematic way of hanging up

→ Either self-centered or too busy

- Documents sent folded

→ Lack of thought for the other party

Arriving at the company:

- Fail to arrive on time

→ fail to read the situation

- Problematic attitude at the reception counter

→ has two faces

- Looks around the company

→ your company is not their first preference

- Do not take off their coats (in winter time)

→ Lacks business manners

2 From their attitude in the waiting room

Keep a discreet eye on them in the waiting room. Where there are multiple applicants in the same room, those who begin to speak in an over friendly manner lack the ability to read the situation. They may lack gravitas about their application because of multiple turndowns from other companies. Both spreading their legs wide apart and crossing their legs is problematic. They may be acting their normal self because they don't realize that they can be seen in the waiting room. These applicants may act humble during the interview. However, as they tend to be double-faced, they will blame their seniors and the company when things aren't going well, causing other workers to lose their motivation. **Those who change their attitude depending on their audience will have difficulty gaining the trust of their colleagues.**

Executive interviews tend to be kept waiting. Check their attitude and facial expression. When the wait is long, hand them a business magazine while apologizing for the wait. Applicants who show no intention of reading the magazine may be too tense, or irritated at being kept waiting. Others might give thanks for the time to relax and breathe. On the other hand, those who have no time to spare will seem irritated and may have problems in cooperativeness. Applicants should not be kept waiting without an explanation, but those applicants who show a severe expression even after receiving an explanation may have difficulties cooperating with others, even though they may be brilliant themselves. It is also problematic to keep them waiting on purpose. Check with the person in charge after interviews for their stress tolerance.

Once the applicant becomes a worker, they won't be able to keep a mask on for long. Every one of us has two-sidedness in us. However, those who let it show fail to do well or fail to stay if they do join the company.

You might be able to see more of an applicant's personality in the waiting room than in an interview.

Attitude in the waiting room:

- Crossing their feet or spreading their feet wide apart, showing a too-confident attitude
- → Two-sided, changes attitudes according to the audience
- Appears to be irritated when they have to wait long
- → Short-tempered, low stress tolerance
- No intention of reading the magazine provided during waiting time

→ may be too full of nerves

- Speaks to other applicants in an over-friendly manner

→ Used to interviews, fails to read the situation

- Frequently checks the time

→ May have another interview ahead of them

3 From their handling of eraser scraps

We can't tell how considerate an applicant is from their academic results or from how they perform in an interview. But we might be able to do so during a writing task.

When getting applicants to do a writing test, look beyond what they write and see how they deal with eraser scraps. There are applicants that are too caught up in writing the test and leave the eraser scraps behind. These applicants may be self-centered and fail to consider others. There are also applicants who gather up their eraser scraps and ask the person in charge about the disposal of rubbish. Those applicants have thought about those who clean up and show they care. There are also applicants who gather their eraser scraps into a pile at the edge of the table. These applicants may lack aggressiveness, but they should be praised for their thoughtfulness. Another type of applicant is the one who sweeps their eraser scraps to the floor so they aren't noticed. These applicants tend to think that things are fine as long as their mistakes aren't noticed. They could be troublemakers. It may be just eraser scraps, but it all counts.

When I talked about this in a seminar, a security

company told me that they also check on applicants' personalities through how they handle eraser scraps.

Check, too, how the applicants hand the test to the applicant behind them before the test starts. There are applicants who want to start as soon as possible, thus passing on the test paper in a rough manner, revealing that they think only of themselves and lack thought for others. A company is no place for solo players; people grow only with the help of others. Self-centered employees have a tendency to fail to obtain help from their surroundings and soon quit the job. **Applicants who hand over the test paper politely, showing consideration for others, are the ones you want. Those who show that they care are bound to grow.**

Ways of handling eraser scraps:

- Sweeps the scraps to the floor
→ May slacken off when people are not noticing
- Leaves the scraps on the desk
→ Lack thoughts for others, self-centered
- Gathers the scraps in a pile on the desk
→ Could be timid, but considerate
- Gathers the scraps and throws them in the bin
→ Decisive, but they should have asked first

- Takes the scraps home
→ Considerate but maybe slightly nervous
- Asks the person in charge about the disposal of scraps
→ Considerate and able to read the situation

4 From their group work (fresh grads)

There are companies that make their final decision through group work during graduate recruiting. Although group work is a way of seeing how applicants interact, it is questionable to rely on it for the final decision. For a start, group work aims at achieving high as a group, and the group's actions depend on its members. Those who play leader in one group may play helper in another group. On the other hand, a good helper member may play leader because of the lack of a leader in their group.

But group work can certainly help. Watch how the members interact. Those who lack cooperation and fail to listen will stay the same and work in the same way after joining your company. Applicants who give up thinking once a problem occurs may be passive and do only what they are told.

As group work is part of the recruiting test, most of the applicants may try their best to speak up and take on the leadership role. Communication skills do not mean being able to give a good speech, or being able to speak up a lot. They are about listening when others speak, showing respect, and building a trusting relationship. A top salesperson may not be a genius with words. They might be quiet, but they understand the customer's needs and are able to give more than what is expected.

There are applicants who unify the group. They tend to listen to every member and lead the group to a conclusion while respecting everyone's ideas. They are the ones who have a high probability of making the right decisions and going far.

Group work allows applicants to be involved in a topic, showing their natural selves. Check if the applicants are considerate of each other, or tend to focus on their own position.

Points to look for during group work:

- See how they cooperate with their group mates
- See if the each member is fulfilling their own responsibilities for their position in the group
- See how they are treated by their other teammates
- See if they are considerate and willing to listen to others
- See if they try to get in the way of others

5 From their greetings, tone of speech and eye contact

Besides what the applicant says, you can check on an applicant's personality through their attitude, facial expression, and tone of voice during an interview. See if they give you a greeting full of spirit. Students who have done mock interviews in their universities tend to give energetic greetings. On the other hand, there are applicants, especially among mid-career applicants, who lack energy and drive. To give a good impression by the way you greet someone is basic behavior for an adult. However, applicants who are finding it difficult to change their career may have lost their confidence, thus they fail to greet with vigor and drive.

You won't feel any vigor unless the applicant means what they say. When you find an applicant simply replaying what they have memorized and rehearsed, encourage them to speak in their own words. It is fine if they really mean what they have rehearsed. But you will not be able to glimpse an applicant's true nature from what they have memorized from an interview guidance book. And again, don't decide to turn someone down just because they aren't speaking in their own words. In order to find the good in the applicant, let them relax and ask them to speak in their own words.

Applicants who end their sentences on a weak note may be lying or trying too hard to look good. On the other hand, those who end their sentences on a strong note may be telling the truth, but they may also be self-centered and unable to appreciate another person's point of view.

Communication ability plays a large role in any job. Those who are able to convey a message or an idea, even though they may not be fabulous in talking, will probably get along with existing clients and staff.

When something seems wrong, try to find the reason and see if the problem can be fixed.

Check the applicant's eye contact as well. When they have no confidence, or when they are lying, they tend to avoid eye contact with the interviewer. When an answer seems suspicious, don't just let it go—dig in deeper. Those who tell the truth will look straight at you. **It is important to judge an applicant's credibility by their eye contact, facial expression, and tone of voice as well as what they say during an interview.** When you ask hesitantly, the applicant is sure to sense your doubt. Listen with interest. Dig in deeper when you find something fishy.

Those who have a serious expression may simply be nervous or lack confidence. It is also possible they haven't formed a good impression of the interviewer.

What to check from the applicant's facial expressions and attitude:

- Greeting lack of spirit
- → Lack of confidence, being turned down for several times
- Avoiding eye contact
- → Lack of confidence. May be lying
- Speaking too softly
- → Lack of confidence
- Speaking out loud
- → Confidence but may be self-centered
- A strict face
- → Nerves, or fail to obtain a good impression

6 From their way of drinking tea

You may not get served with tea while recruiting for fresh graduates, but it is common to get tea during an individual interview for mid-career recruits. Check how they drink their tea when they are served it. Those who forgot their Ps and Qs lack business manners, or they may just be very nervous. Those who drink their tea without a word may lack business manners, or they may have a very self-centered working style.

It may seem a small thing if the applicant says "thank you", but it shows the applicant has the ability to be considerate of others. They will cooperate with their co-workers and people who work under them.

Those who refuse to drink their tea may be nervous, but they may also be not quite convinced by the interview itself. The same can also be said in a trade or sales environment. If a customer refuses to drink the tea served, there is usually no sale, no deal. Those who take only one single sip may be either fussy or inconsiderate. We cannot deny the possibility of them neglecting the tea due to their nerves or being caught up in a conversation. However, if they want to make a good impression on the interviewer, the applicant will usually finish their tea.

During interviews for mid-career recruitments, don't think of the interview as a plain interview. Think of the applicants as salespersons who have come to promote themselves to the company. **Try to present an environment in which the salesperson can make their pitch over a cup of tea instead of in a sterile environment. That way you can get to hear more of the applicant's own words.**

Applicants are choosing the company that they want to join. If they form a good impression of the interviewer they will develop a strong will to join the company. They will want to build a connection over a cup of tea. No matter how much experience they have had in the world, those who fail to connect with the interviewer will probably develop problems with the current staff.

It may just be a cup of tea, but it is a great tool for glimpsing what type of person the applicant is.

How they react to a cup of tea:

- Says nothing to the staff that distributes the tea
→ Too nervous or lacks business manners

- Drinks the tea without a greeting

$\rightarrow$ Either has no time to spare or is self-centered

- Refuses to drink the tea

$\rightarrow$ Low willingness to enter the company

- Takes only a single sip

$\rightarrow$ Inconsiderate. No time to spare or the tea may be distasteful

- Pleasantly drinks the tea

$\rightarrow$ Makes a good impression on the interviewer, strong will to join company

7 From their of leaving the room

Check on the applicant's facial expression and attitude as they leave the room after the interview. You don't need to pay much attention to those you don't intend to take on. However, focus on those you would like to make an offer to. Check if they are satisfied with the interview and have a strong desire to join the company; otherwise, they may turn down the offer later.

It is common to think that it is the company who is choosing their staff, but the applicants are also choosing the company. People with high capability will be in demand. An interview is not only a tool to look closely at an applicant—it is also a chance to entice the applicant into your company.

Those who have a low intention of joining your company will tend not to make eye contact with the interviewer during the last greeting before they leave. No "Thank you for your time" and no vigor in their farewell. On the other hand, applicants with a strong desire to join the company will be sure to give an energetic "Thank you very much."

Applicants who leave quickly may be showing their low

intention of joining the company. **Applicants who greet the interviewer before the interview but not after may not be satisfied with the interview.**

It is important to explain and have the applicant understand the true working conditions and workload of the position. However, if the interviewer puts too much emphasis on the negatives, no one will want to work for the company. The applicant will feel much better if you add that the problems are improving and that you hope to make the company better with the help of the applicant.

Presentation does affect the way applicants think about the company. Therefore, try to conduct the interview in a way that will make the applicant feel positive about working in your company.

When you find an applicant leaving unsatisfied, you should find out the reason for it. Sometimes it is nothing major—it might be just something the interviewer said that caused the applicant to feel doubtful about working for your company. Therefore, aftercare is important, especially when someone you would like to recruit starts acting strangely.

There are interviewers who check on the applicant's intentions just before the applicant leaves the room. This could be counter-productive. Do not ask directly, "Would you accept an offer if I give you one?" because if you force them to make a speech about their intentions, the applicant may think that you are so in need of new staff that you will take simply anyone.

Attitude that show that the applicant is not interested:

- Greetings with no vigor
- Leaving quickly
- Not looking at the interviewer
- No farewell as they leave the room

Column 4

First impressions

During my seminars targeted at HR personnel, I often tell them not to judge a book by its cover. However, many interviewers, even the most experienced, tend to judge a person based on their first impressions of them. I once participated in a television show to find out the "real" as a guest professional. On my first attempt, I got it totally wrong. I had made the mistake of making my decision based on the first impression obtained. Even after going to so many interviews, I am still unable to determine what sort of person someone is simply by the first impression they give. Sometimes we do make mistakes. There are no people who are the same. Every applicant we meet is a complete stranger, and we should not judge them based on other people we have met before. (By the way, I successfully identified the target on my second attempt on the television show.)

CHAPTER 5

ASK THE STANDARD
QUESTIONS

The standard questions you will ask in an interview relate to the applicant's reason for applying, their self-evaluation, their strengths and weaknesses, their school or academic life (for fresh grads), their job history (for mid-career recruits), and their reason for leaving their previous job (for mid-career recruits). Depending on the responses you get, you can ask further questions based on these themes. Consider also asking questions "with a twist"—i.e. something that the applicant might not be expecting.

1 Reason for applying

The reason for applying is one of the questions that all of the applicants should have thought through. They should have an answer ready. There is nothing wrong with a prepared answer as long as it is based on facts. However, if the applicant lies in the hope of getting an offer, mismatching could result.

The main points to consider when looking at their stated reasons for applying are **their motivation for this type of work, the skills and aptitude they want to leverage in your company and the reasons for specifically wanting to work for your company.** If the reasons given are vague and can be applied to any company, the applicant may have a low willingness to join your company. Even if they end up joining your company, they may fail to stay.

For fresh graduate applicants, because they don't have much formal work experience, their motive for applying will tend to be based on what they have learnt from school or their part-time job experiences. Passion and aspiration are the main factors you are looking for in fresh grads.

On the other hand, it would be unwise to give an offer to a mid-career applicant based purely on their aspiration and passion. Look instead for answers that show the applicant's ability to self-analyze and understand the abilities and experiences they can apply to the job. These are the people who will become good workers. Even when they apply for job where they have no experience, please check if they are able to show that they have related skills and that they are willing to acquire the skills and knowledge they lack.

If the applicant only wants to put what they have learnt into practice, they can pretty much do that in any company. The key factor to look for is whether the applicant has done enough background research to grasp the characteristics of your company and to base their reasons on that. Applicants who want to join the company based on current good business results may end up leaving the company when the company has a bad year. So if their reasons include such praise of your company as 'Top class in the field" or 'The products are excellent," they are focusing on the hard work of existing staff and may have a passive working style. When the applicant lists what they want to do, ask them about what they have done to achieve their goal. Applicants who have more than just passion—those who can give an answer based on imagining their working selves in your company—are the ones who seriously want to join your company.

Check on their facial expressions when they give an answer. When applicants speak from the heart, you will find no dullness in their eyes. The interviewer will surely feel their passion.

Points to look for from the reason for applying:

- See if they can put their experience to work
- See if they have a specific reason for wanting to join your company
- See if you can feel passion and willingness from their facial expressions when they give their answers

Questions branched out from the reason of application:

- What is the career goal you wish to achieve?
- What can you only achieve in our company?
- What do you think you should do to achieve your goals?
- How did you research our company?

2 Self-evaluation

The key factor to look for in an applicant's self-evaluation is what they can put into practice in your company. You can also find the applicant's passion towards work and their desire to enter your company from their self-evaluation.

During recruitment for fresh graduates, check out what they are capable of doing based on what they have learnt as a student or from working part-time, even though they may not have much working experience. For mid-career recruits, check the applicant's working ability closely, looking for transferrable skills and knowledge. **Applicants who are unable to understand what type of person the company is after will give vague answers.** They fail to give an impression that they would come in much use. If the applicants are able to list specific examples and show how their working abilities would benefit the company, they are the ones you should be after.

See if their self-evaluation mainly consists of bragging about their achievements, rather than giving you an idea of what they could achieve in your company.

Check on the applicant's communication skills. See if they are able to present well what they want to say. Answers with the conclusion at the start of the pitch will give the interviewers a basic understanding of what the applicant intends to say even if they stuff up later on. Some applicants speak with passion. However, even though we can understand their passion, we might not understand all the other things they present, especially when they put the conclusion at the end of their pitch. The applicant's self-evaluation may end up being just a long speech with no main point.

Give the applicant a time limit to present their self-evaluation. By asking the applicant to give a one-minute pitch, you can check fluency and time management, as well as content.

Ask those applicants who fail to give specific examples of their experience to add examples to their pitch. This will increase their credibility. Everyone can brag about something, but don't trust every word they say if they fail to backup their claims with examples. Consider how you can test the applicant's ability and credibility as you listen to their pitch.

Points to look for from their self-evaluation:

- If their ability is beneficial to the company
- If the pitch is based on experience
- If the pitch is just bragging talk or not
- The applicant's communication skills

Questions that branch from self-evaluation:

- Give some specific examples
- How are you able to leverage in our company?
- What did everyone say about your ability?
- Give me a pitch on something other than your school life

3 Strengths and weaknesses

When you ask about the applicant's strengths and weaknesses, all you will get are prepared answers. **Check if they have based their answers on their experiences, giving examples.** If they give a vague answer, it is fine to ask for examples during the interview. Make sure that the strengths the applicant lists are skills that can be used in your company. Ask about how they can leverage their strengths if they work in your company. If you have already asked questions about their self-evaluation, ask about their personality and actions while digging into their strengths.

As for their weaknesses, try to see if a weakness is likely to cause problems in your company. If they are short tempered, for example, it may cause troubles with customers and colleagues. If they don't stick to anything, they may not stick to the job and resign later. Therefore, think about how their weaknesses would affect their working behavior. It is also important to see how the applicants understand their weaknesses and if they are trying to improve. Those who give up just because they can't do much about their weaknesses would do the same in the workplace. They will simply give up on work they can't do instead of trying to improve themselves. Applicants who are aware of their weaknesses and are trying to find a remedy are the ones to look out for.

Rarely do we see applicants who say they don't have weaknesses. Such applicants are problematic—not only can they not self-analyze, they may also be self-centered and fail to treat problems as problems. Fresh grad applicants who cannot see their own faults may not be ready to receive advice from senior staff and cause problems as a result.

Do not just listen when the applicant talks about their strengths and weaknesses. Dig in deeper and lead the conversation. Interviewers who try to dig in deeper leave a good impression with the applicants. By being interested in the applicant and asking questions repeatedly will lead you to knowing the applicant's true self.

Points to look for from the strengths and weaknesses:

- If their strengths are beneficial to the company
- If their weaknesses are likely to cause problems to their work
- If they are trying to improve their weaknesses
- If their answers are credible

Questions that branch from the strengths and weaknesses:

- Give an example from your experience that explains your strengths
- How would you put your strengths to work?
- Have your weaknesses ever affected your work?
- Are you trying to overcome your weaknesses?

4 School / academic life (fresh grads)

When recruiting for fresh graduates, ask about what they have done during their years at school. In this way **you will be able to see connections to work, their understanding of boss–subordinate relationships, their goal-achievement ability, their communication skills, their tolerance of stress,** and other characteristics. Of course, the applicants will have prepared for this question, so dig in deeper to check their credibility instead of just listening.

When you get an answer that focuses exclusively on their experience of club activities and part-time work, ask them about their academic life as well. Vice versa, ask about their club activities and casual work experience if they only describe their academic life. Although applicants who have been trying hard in the academic field are respectful, you need to make sure they are ready for your company. If they graduated from a degree with a completely irrelevant major, ask them their reason for applying to your company. If they answer that it is hard to get a job in their own field, the applicant will be unlikely to stay even if they receive an offer.

Those who have been through club activities and casual jobs will have a good understanding of boss–subordinate relationships, and will be able to build good relationships with their seniors and colleagues. On the other hand, those who have focused only on their academic life will likely be problematic in human relationships, causing them to be less likely to grow within the company. Ask for the specifics of working periods and work content while asking about the applicant's job experiences. Some applicants stress their short-term work experiences because they don't have anything else to talk about. Double-check the credibility of the content.

Regarding club activities, ask the applicant about the role they played in the club and how they would put their experience to work in your company. Applicants who have been working hard in club activities will be able to give specific examples.

Those who have nothing to say about their school life probably have no goals and aims. Such applicants may be applying only because it is the time for getting a job. Applicants who have nothing to share when asked for specific episodes are applicants who have achieved nothing through their school life.

Points to look for from their academic life (fresh grads):

- If they had a goal
- If their academic and part-time work experiences are beneficial to the company
- If they are able to supply episodes and if the episodes are credible
- If they can handle boss–subordinate relationships

Questions that branch from their academic life (fresh grads):

- How would you make the best of your experience?
- Did you experience problems related to personal relationships during club activities?
- What from your casual work experience can you leverage into work?
- Are you not interested in the field you have worked casually for?

5 Job history (mid-career)

Just as you checked out the fresh graduates' academic life, check out the relevance of the mid-career applicants' job history, and what sort of experiences they have had.

See from the applicant's job history if they are answering based on the understanding of what your company is after and what they have to give. If they just seem to be reading out what they have on their résumé, they have not grasped what they have to give. If the applicant is changing jobs a lot, they may be a passive worker. **They may be unable to appeal to the strengths and abilities they have acquired from experience.**

For mid-career applicants, the applicant's job history will have a huge influence on the final decision. Even if the applicant has worked in one of the finest companies, they will not integrate well with existing staff and may leave your company if they lack the experience and ability needed for the job.

Double-check on the credibility of the applicant's job history. If the applicant fails to give examples of their achievements, avoids eye contact, or shows signs of lacking confidence, you should be doubtful about their credibility. There are also applicants who tend to focus on the experience wanted even though they haven't done much in the field. Ask for specific achievements and what they have specifically done.

Those who keep talking about their job history lack the understanding of what they want to say. It depends on the applicants' experience, but if they fail to finish their answer in one minute, they are probably just giving you a list of all their job experiences.

If the applicant fails to volunteer what they can do for you company, based on their previous experience, ask them outright. Check the applicant's facial expression and eye contact as they answer your questions. Applicants who lack confidence will speak softly and avoid eye contact.

While recruiting mid-career, usually you will be looking for people who can become solid performers within a short time. You should not hire someone simply for their personality or passion. Listen to how the applicant is willing to work and benefit the company based on their experience. Check on what they answer and their facial expressions while they talk.

Points to look for from their job history (mid-career):

- If they understand the work type wanted for your company
- If they are able to stress experience related to the position
- If they have included achievements in their answer
- If you can see their confidence while they give their answer

Questions that branch from their job history (mid-career):

- Give me specific examples of something you have achieved
- We have a unique working style. Are you okay with that?
- Is it fine that we are in a different working field?
- Do you have any management experience?

6 Reason for leaving (mid-career)

There are a lot of possible reasons for leaving a job. If the applicant claims that they left the job for personal reasons, probe deeper. If they left because of a lack of working ability, they may still feel bad and not want to talk about it.

If the applicant left their former job just to get away from the conditions there, history might repeat itself in your company. Applicants who repeatedly change careers may still be unsatisfied and in search of a job they want to do.

No matter the actual reason for leaving—whether it be failure to get along with their colleagues, not getting the compliments they think they deserved, bad working conditions, not being treated well, or any other reason—there are applicants that hide the facts because they fear they will reflect badly on their profile, even if they were not at fault. Therefore, question them whenever you feel a doubt. Applicants who are not satisfied with the conditions they had before may be changing careers simply for the working conditions.

If the applicant was at fault, they will think it a negative factor and try to hide the fact. For applicants over 30 who left owing to bad performance, ask how they have tried to improve their performance since. If they treat having a bad performance report as something not related to them, such applicants may lack responsibility as well as working ability.

For applicants who are aiming to change careers by leaving their current workplace, double-check on their reasons. Those applicants who want to change jobs because they have been treated unfairly, or something unpleasant has occurred, may be stopped by their current company, which may attempt to make amends. Therefore, they might turn down your offer.

You should see if the reason the applicant left their former workplace might repeat itself in your company. However, do not get too caught up with the past and ignore what the applicant has to offer now. Do not focus the whole interview on the reason for leaving the former job. Some applicants left their former company because they felt thwarted—they could not use their talents. If your company is able to give them the opportunity to use their talents, this links up to their reason for applying. You can expect such applicants to flourish.

Points to look for from their reasons for leaving (mid-career):

- If they left their former job just because they didn't like it
- If they have settled their emotions after leaving their job at the former company's convenience
- If they easily use "bad sales" as a reason
- If they are able to link up their reasons for leaving and reasons for applying

Questions that branch from their reasons of leaving (mid-career):

- Will you leave our company for the same reason?
- I don't seem to read a flow in your past jobs
- Were you unable to do so in your former workplace?
- Why are you changing jobs in the same work field?

7 Give the standard questions a twist

By simply giving a twist to the standard questions (i.e. questions related to reasons for applying, self-evaluation, job history, and reasons for leaving the former workplace), you can prevent the applicant from using prepared answers and get them to speak off-the-cuff. Therefore, try asking the standard questions in a slightly different way.

[A Twist on reasons for applying]
Why us out of all the other companies out there?

This question asks for more than just the reasons for applying. It also requires an understanding of other companies based on thorough background research. The applicant will not be able to answer the question if they lack understanding of either factor. If they give a vague answer, either they haven't done enough background research, or they don't have a strong will to join your company.

Why did you apply to us, a company that is in the same field as your former company? (mid-career)

Even though you can expect the applicant to become a good worker straightaway, you still need to know why they have changed jobs within the same work fields. A good answer is one that explains the difference between your company and the applicant's former workplace, and outlines what the applicant can do in your company that they cannot do in their former workplace.

Are you applying for companies offering similar jobs?

By understanding the ranking of your company within the work field, you will be able to see the applicant's willingness to join your company. As for the applicants who say that your company is their first choice, make sure you ask for the reason your company is their first choice. You will be able to see if the applicant really understands your company and what they can do in your company.

[A Twist on self-evaluation]

Give me a self-evaluation for what you can do only in our company.

Most of the applicants will have an answer ready for a standard question about their self-evaluation. However, they will be confused when the question is a bit twisted. They will need to think and answer in their own words. They will need to pull out information from their brains and give you real answers instead of answers they have memorized beforehand.

Try to promote yourself as if you are a product for sale.

The required content for the question is the same as for a normal self-evaluation. The twist is that applicants need to think of what to say about themselves as a product for sale. They will need to try to attract the interest of the interviewers, and they will need to have the communication ability to treat the interviewers as customers.

Give me an example of a strength you can leverage in our company.

When the applicant is restricted to one strength, they will need to think about which one to select. A plain answer will fail to leave an impression on the interviewer. Applicants who have a strong understanding of their strengths will be able to understand the interviewer's intentions and give an answer to this twisted question.

[A Twist on job history (or academic life)]
Tell me about yourself.

Fresh graduates should be able to give a simple summary of their life and interests. Mid-career applicants may focus on their job history, but if they say nothing more than their name and name of the company they worked for, you can conclude that they have nothing positive to say about themselves.

Tell me about one thing you can do best for the company based on your strengths and experience.

Applicants who do not understand their own strengths will not be able to give a specific answer to this question. You

ASK THE STANDARD | CHAPTER
QUESTIONS | 5

can expect an answer about the one thing they are able to do best. If they answer directly, instead of twisting and turning, you will be able to understand the working ability of the applicant.

Explain your job history in one minute.

See if the applicant is able to give the highlights of their experience within a short timeframe. If the applicant tends to babble on and drag it out, they will do the same at work. On the other hand, applicants that end far short of the one-minute limit may not have the depth of working experience required.

[A twist on reasons for leaving]
Did you leave your prior jobs on good terms?

There are few applicants who say they left with a fuss. However, the process may not have been pleasant if they show a gloomy face for even a split second. There may be a problem with their working ability, especially if they left the working place after a short time.

So you left the company because of bad sales. What did you do to improve the situation? (mid-career)

There are a lot of applicants who claim to have left their former workplace because of bad sales. If the applicant is over 30 years of age, check if they have done something since to try to improve the matter. If they tend to think it is the others to blame, the applicant may lack a sense of responsibility and you can't expect much from their working ability either.

Explain your reason for leaving simply. (mid-career)

For applicants who have changed jobs many times, you should check on their reasons for leaving each of their prior jobs just in case. If they keep giving the simple answer "personal reasons," there may be a problem on their side that led to leaving each job, and history could repeat itself.

Points to look for from twisted standard questions:

- If they are speaking the truth by changing the question
- If they leave a good impression by their facial expressions and tone of speech while answering
- If they can adapt to change

Column 5

Pros and cons of standard questions

Applicants would have come prepared for standard questions, such as questions about their intentions for applying and their self-evaluation. You are not able to make a judgment about hiring the applicant based purely on these model answers. Interviewers who find it unfair to ask different questions to different applicants would be repeating the same set of questions over and over again—every applicant is different, so it makes sense to ask them different questions.

Even when asking standard questions, you will get different answers just by giving the question a twist. It makes it harder for an interviewer to make the right decision when they are repeating the same questions for every interview they conduct. It is important to be conscious about the conversational flow. Be interested in the applicants' answers and ask them questions that show you want to hear more from them. Applicants who feel your interest will start to speak in their own words. If you just ask the standard questions, an interview will be no more than a document check.

CHAPTER 6

ASK MORE SPECIFIC QUESTIONS

This chapter provides some specific questions designed to give you an insight into applicants' working abilities and aptitudes in different fields—desk jobs, sales jobs, shop assistants, technical jobs, manufacturing jobs, and jobs in management. It then gives suggestions for some surprise questions you could ask the applicants, or questions to hone in on their communication skills, or to probe sensitive areas. It concludes by looking at the sorts of insights you can gain from the questions applicants ask you.

1 Desk jobs (job-related questions)

Why did you choose this job?

This question looks at the applicant's vision as an office worker, thus determining how earnest they are about a desk job.

It is doubtful that the applicant will become a good worker if they have applied for the job just so they don't have to become a salesperson or shop assistant. It is not only computer skills and languages that count. Knowledge of managerial, human resource, and general fields—and also how they feel about working in a desk job—should be points to look for from their answers.

If you fail to get a clear response to this question, the applicant may not be passionate about the job at all. They may simply be in a position where they need to find a job somewhere. Those who wish to do desk jobs would appeal to their attempts to increase their skills for the job through self-development courses.

Office jobs provide support and backup for other departments. Therefore, make sure that the applicant does not just do as they are told passively. Check on their problem-solving skills as well.

Checkpoints:

- Are the applicants applying because they dislike other types of jobs?
- Do they have the skills and knowledge for the job?
- Do they have a communication problem?
- Do they have a vision for their future?

We sometimes transfer our clerks to the sales department. Are you fine with that?

It is important to make it clear to the applicant that transfers are commonplace. If they are uncomfortable with that, you should not give them an offer.

When there is no working experience to refer to for fresh graduates, there's a good chance that in the future workers will be transferred to other departments according to their abilities, even though they may have been hired as a clerk in the first place. On the other hand, mid-career employees may be employed for their specialty based on their experience. However, they may be too attached to a specific job type. Those who insist on a particular job type may not be thinking of work as a contribution to the company. They may be self-centered and only do the work they want to do.

The applicant should give an answer describing their strengths and passion in relation to the job. They should also be willing to take on the challenge of transferring between departments. If the applicant seems unsure and asks, "Were you not recruiting for office workers?," they may have problems getting along with the existing staff and dealing with stress. Check their willingness to work as part of a team.

Checkpoints:

- Are they ready to work for the company's benefit?
- Do they have a one-sided view about the job type?
- Are they applying for office work for an easy job?
- Are they showing dissatisfaction through their actions and expressions?

What skills do you think are required for a clerical job?

Even for the same job type, every position is recruiting for a different type of person. Therefore, check how much study the applicant has done of your company. If the applicant really wants to work in a clerical job, they will be able to talk specifically about what they want to do and what they will do. If you are recruiting for fresh graduates, vague answers can be expected. However, you should be able to find some concrete answers on the applicant's abilities based on whatever experience they have had.

Office jobs play an important role in backing-up and supporting sales and other staff in the field. If the applicant is applying just because they want to work in the head office, they may not be qualified for the job.

What we should be after is someone who wants to contribute to the company using their skills and knowledge, and someone who is trying to solve problems and make things work. There are no model answers for this question. However, the applicant's response will show whether they really want to work as a clerk and if they know what they are expected to do.

Checkpoints:

- Do they match up with the person you are after for the position?
- Do they have an understanding about backing-up and supporting other departments?
- Do they answer with a clear future vision?
- Are they thinking with a mindset to make things happen?

Tell me your strengths that can benefit our company.

This question is suitable for applicants who are applying mid-career. If the applicant has not thought about the type of person the company is recruiting for and gives an answer purely based on their own experience, their answer will have no impact. Mid-career recruits are expected to become part of the workforce quickly. Different skills are required for different departments. For example, the HR department may be hiring for someone to deal with their practical work, such as payrolls and social insurance procedures. At the same time, the same department might be after someone who is good at personnel and recruitment strategies. Therefore, it is important to not just read what is on their résumé. Ask them to tell you about their ability and get some concrete examples of what they can do.

When asked this question, those who are not sure of what abilities are wanted will give vague answers. Do not hire someone who says: "I don't know until I start working in the company." Mid-career recruits who become good workers are able to understand what they should do through recruitment ads and interviews.

Checkpoints:

- Do they match up with what your company is after?
- Do they give solid answers?

- Can they tell you what they are expected to do?
- Do you feel that they are ready for the job?

2 Sales jobs (job-related questions)

Tell me about your strengths as a salesperson. (fresh grads)

See if the applicant is giving you an answer based on their research about sales jobs. Applicants who are able to self-analyze will be able to appeal to the skills and abilities they are able to utilize based on their experience working part-time. Those who are having difficulty finding a job, and have decided that it would be easy to get a sales job, will not be able to give a persuasive response. Applicants who lack passion and willingness will not do well, even if they end up being hired. Those who do not give a sincere answer may shift responsibility when they have low sales. Those who really want to work as a salesperson will be able to imagine what they will be doing and link it to their strengths during their self-evaluation. Follow up on this question by asking about their supporting experience. Salespeople represent the whole company because they deal directly with customers. Make sure the applicant is persuasive and able to leave a good overall impression.

Checkpoints:

- Are they able to self-analyze?
- Do they have an understanding about sales jobs?
- Were they able to give a persuasive answer?
- Is their answer based on their own experience?

What type of person do your peers see you as?

This is a question that involves a third-party's remarks. Sales jobs require the ability to negotiate with people. If the applicant does not have many friends, or is unable to tell how their peers see them, the applicant may have problems developing relationships with others.

Applicants who are able to give an answer straightaway have a good relationship with their peers, and are the ones that are likely to stay in the company. Applicants who fail to have frequent communication with their peers are not expected to be able to achieve in an aggressive area such as sales. Sales customers are also people. Applicants who are able to build good relationships may become good workers. In jobs that serve individual customers, the applicant's peers may become customers. Thus it may not be a good idea to hire someone with no friends.

This question can also be asked in relation to other

job positions in order to check on the applicants' personal relationships. Follow up this question with an inquiry about the communication they share with their peers. What a third-party says about the applicant may be more credible than a self-evaluation.

Checkpoints:

- Know the number of peers as well as their remarks
- Check if the applicant is able to build good relationships
- Be doubtful about the applicants' personal relationships when you receive a vague answer
- Ask about the type of peers the applicant mostly has

How can you utilize your experience as a salesperson in our company? (mid-career)

Ask mid-career applicants with experience in sales to list what they are able to do. If this is not done right, even the most experienced may turn out to be mismatched after they join the company. Explain your company's situation and ask for solid answers.

When recruiting for a sales position, be wary of those who use impressive vocabulary. If they have no achievements to back up their words, their fine vocabulary will not contribute much. Applicants who utilize their experience and have a concrete image of sales in mind are eager to work and will be able to join the workforce immediately. On the other hand, applicants that are not so eager, or work in a passive way, will reply that they will think about it after they join the company. Sales positions are aggressive jobs, so check if the applicant is able to make things happen. If they come from a different field, ask the applicant how they are prepared to deal with the different type of merchandise. Research is crucial when it comes to sales jobs. Make sure the applicant has done thorough research on the company that they are applying for.

Checkpoints:

- Are they answering with an understanding of your company?
- Do they know what they should do?
- Are their achievements credible?
- Do they have problems with different knowledge needed for different fields?

Tell me about the difficult times you have had as a salesperson. (mid-career)

Most applicants will talk about their successes, not their failures or any difficulties that they have encountered.This is natural, but it is through knowing how they deal with the failures and difficulties that you will be able to assess their working ability and problem-solving skills. The answer to this question may also serve as reference to decide if the applicant has the ability to deal with the problems that happen in your company.

When you find applicants taking the issue as their own problem, even if they were not the cause of the trouble, you have found responsible applicants with potential. On the other hand, those who blame others and babble on and on are not aware that the cause of the problem is their lack of management skill. When trouble is caused for a customer, it is the salesperson's responsibility even though they may not have caused it. Dig into the real self of the applicant by asking questions they have not prepared for.

Checkpoints:

- Did they blame others for the troubles?
- Do they treat the episode as a lesson to learn from?
- Do they have problems when dealing with stress?
- Are they giving credible answers?

3 Shop assistant and manager jobs (job-related questions)

Have you been to one of our stores?

When an applicant wishes to work in a store, it would be strange if they have never been to one of the stores of the company that they are applying for—this links to their eagerness to work in the company. There are times when an applicant is unable to go to the store for an interview because of the store's location. It is understandable for the applicant's first interview, but make sure the applicant gets a chance to go to the store if they proceed further in the recruitment process. Follow up this question with an inquiry about what they thought of the merchandise and services of the store. Ask for details about the store the applicant has been to in order to increase their credibility. Ask not only what they saw, but also what they felt could be improved. Applicants who say there is nothing to improve are problematic, but those who go on forever about points to improve are no better and could be regarded as tactless.

It is crucial that all staff in the store have the ability to present their thoughts without giving a negative impression to their target audience. Some applicants focus on the geographical location instead of the layout of goods and customer service, or any points related to the job. Those applicants may turn out to blame others when things go wrong.

Checkpoints:

- Can they think of points to improve, based on their own judgment?
- Do they have a lively expression when they talk?
- Do they understand the attractive features of your company?
- What reaction did they give if they had not been to a store before?

Do you have experience working as a shop manager? (mid-career)

When hiring full-time staff, you need to check not only their sales experience, but also their management skills when it comes to staff and merchandise. If the applicant claims to have managerial experience, check their specific involvement and ask them what they would do to increase the sales. An experienced shop manager will be able to give you a credible answer about how to serve customers and close sales based on their own experience. Follow up this question by asking the applicant what type of shop manager they want to become. For those who have no managerial experience, ask them about their experience teaching new staff. If they have had experience teaching new staff, they will know what they are expected to do as a shop assistant. Ask about their ways of teaching and their achievements as well.

To become the head manager of the store, not only knowledge of the merchandise and the ability to sell are required, but also the ability to lead staff and work as part of a team. Ask the applicant for solid examples of this as they give their answers. Furthermore, ask them about how they would like to manage a store.

Checkpoints:

- Do you see leadership in them?
- Are the applicants all on the right track?
- Do they have ideas to increase sales?
- Do they look lively as they speak?

4 Technical jobs (job-related questions)

How would you utilize the skills you have learnt? (fresh grads)

When recruiting fresh grads, check how they plan to utilize the skills and knowledge they gained from their academic life. A science student, for example, should be able to link their studies to a relevant aspect of the job they are applying for. However, if they give a vague answer, they may have failed to understand the work content or be doubtful about their knowledge and skills. For technical jobs, applicants with the experience of programming and those who do not will differ largely in the time they need to become part of the workforce. Do not dismiss what they have learnt at school or university—try to find parts of it that can be utilized in your company.

Some technician students are still struggling about whether they should continue their studies or not. If they are the ones you are looking for, try to give them a concrete image of themselves using what they have learnt by bringing it to the field. Do not dismiss any answer the applicant gives. Let them feel your empathy and show them the skills they can use. On top of that, outline for them a possible career path in your company.

Checkpoints:

- Do they have the skills needed?
- Are they eager to join the company?
- Does anything stand out from what they have done back in school?
- How keen are they on technician jobs?

Would you mind telling me about your job-hunting situation? (mid-career)

Other companies besides your own are after ace technicians. This question does not only check whether the applicant is applying to other companies, it also helps you find the ranking of your own company when the applicant is applying for several other positions. If the answer you get is, "Your company is my first choice," ask the applicant for their reasons for treating your company as their first choice. If they are able to give a clear, detailed answer, their response is credible. However, vague answers such as "having a high-level of technology", or "offering a prosperous future," may show that the applicant is still thinking about it. If they are good technicians, the interviewer should explain to them the level of your company and what role they would be able to play. This is also a good time to explain the position in detail, including the working conditions.

To recruit high-quality staff, the interviewer must have spectacular negotiation skills. Explain to the applicant sincerely that they are people that your company needs. Specific knowledge and skills are often required during an interview for technical jobs. Consider inviting people from the department to join in the interview.

Checkpoints:

- Is your company on the top of their list?
- Do they understand the attractive features of your company?
- Is there a problem with the wages and working conditions?
- Are they certain that they want to change jobs if they are currently working?

Where do you want to be in five years' time as a technician?

This question is designed to see if they have vision as a technician. If what they picture differs from your company's aims, mismatching may occur after the applicant joins your company. You need to explain the situation clearly at the time of recruiting, especially to dispatched workers who stay in the consignee company. They may imagine themselves being an

SE (system engineer) after five years, but your company may not offer such positions.

Mid-career applicants may be aiming at becoming project leaders or managers. However, if the applicant is not capable of becoming so, they may end up being unwanted staff. Double-check your HR strategies before you make a decision.

If you are hiring them for a full-time job, you must not just look at the job right in front of you. It is very important to check if the applicant's vision is possible to fulfill elsewhere in your company.

Checkpoints:

- Is it possible to fulfill the applicant's vision in your company?
- Are they just fantasizing about the job, and do they have the capability?
- Can they put their managerial skills to work?
- Are you looking at this with a global view?

Do you have experience in being a leader? (mid-career)

Make sure you double-check the projects the applicant has been involved in. No matter the period of involvement, if the applicants' experiences are all group experiences, they may be deficient in leadership or technical skills. Those who simply give as an answer "No, I have no experience" may lack eagerness to enter the company and become a leader. Those who lack experience but are eager will state that they have experience in supporting leaders and that they are eager to try working in a leadership role. As a lot of teamwork is involved in technical jobs, an applicant's leadership and management skills need to be looked at before hiring them full time. Find the type of person you need through asking this question. Credit should be given to those who try to give a good response. Dig deeper into those who have experience as a leader and ask about their attitude as a leader. Remember to double-check their credibility.

Checkpoints:

- Are they giving solid, credible episodes when answering the question?
- Even if they are inexperienced, have they played an assistant role to the leader?
- Can you see leadership potential from their answer?
- Can their experience be used in your company?

5 Manufacturing jobs (job-related questions)

Why do you want to work in the manufacturing area? (fresh grads)

When recruiting for fresh grads, applicants who are able to link up their experience and knowledge to the field while answering this question should be given credit for their passion. If they do not, check why the applicant has become interested in making things and manufacturing as a whole.

Some applicants apply for a job in manufacturing for reasons such as being shy or needing a stable job. Those people will not be able to blend in. They may find other jobs to be much more interesting and fail to stay. Applicants who give a simple answer but mean what they say are the people you want. There are also applicants who simply repeat the same words that senior staff members have presented during the information session. If they cannot put the points into their own words, you should be doubtful about their understanding. Even though some applicants may not speak poetry, they mean every word they say, and you will feel the weight in each word. Such applicants speak passionately about their eagerness to work in the manufacturing field.

Checkpoints:

- Are you persuaded by their reasons?
- Do you sense the passion from their speech?
- Are they just trying to get away from becoming a salesperson?
- Can they use what they have learnt in the past?

How do you picture the future of the manufacturing business in Japan?

An experienced manufacturing worker should be able to passionately describe their vision for the future of the industry. Check if the applicant is able to see the negatives as well as the positives, and if they can suggest solutions to the negatives. By asking this question, you will be able to assess if the applicant has passion and vision.

Instead of being negative about the industry shifting overseas, applicants who are able to see the possibilities of Japan winning the global race by increasing their creative skills will have a broad, prospective overview of the industry. Such applicants also have problem-solving skills.

Ask this question along with another question on what the manufacturing industry should do in order to grow. The answer to this follow-up question will show whether the applicant has an understanding of the type of manufacturing company your company is. The applicants who are eager to join the company will know what is expected of them. From the applicant's answer to this question, check for passion and eagerness to employ in your company the manufacturing skills the applicant has already acquired.

Checkpoints:

- Did applicants understand the situation and give a credible answer?
- Are they willing to overcome problems?
- Can they take things in a positive manner?
- Did they answer with an understanding of what they can do for your company?

6   Managerial jobs

Tell me your strengths as a manager and the number of subordinates you have had. (mid-career)

Unless they understand the situation your company is in, and can earn the trust of your existing staff, it is hard to get new managerial staff to stay long enough to show what they can do. A lot of the applicants apply because of the attractive labor conditions on offer. Try to assess their managerial ability by asking them this open-ended question. If they give vague answers such as, "building a trust relationship with my subordinates", or "gather the department as one," ask for specific examples of what they have done in the past. Those who have mastered managerial skills will be able to give you a concrete answer based on solid examples, or even their achievements and results obtained.

You should also check the number of subordinates the applicant has had in the past. It does not mean that the applicant has fewer managerial skills when they have a smaller team, but it is dangerous to hire someone just by looking at their job title. There are people applying for managerial jobs who have had only one single subordinate in their previous experience. Unless the person has legitimate managerial skills and earns the trust of existing staff, they will not be able to unite the department as one. Check on the personality and working style of the applicant as a managerial officer as they answer this question.

Checkpoints:

- Are their strengths based on solid experience?
- Is there a problem with them having only a small number of subordinates?
- Are they able to earn the trust of existing staff?
- Do they understand what they should do as a manager?

Tell me an episode of failure as a manager. (mid-career)

Those who are hired plainly for their past glory may not blend into your workforce in the end. It is problematic when the applicant appeals to their achievements and results, displaying an absence of humility. When an applicant tells you that they have never failed (showing you a highhanded attitude), you should not hire them. Those who share their past mistakes and have learnt humbly from those mistakes are the ones to look for.

Being humble and understanding others' feelings are skills that a manager needs to have. If the applicant fails to identify failure as failure, or starts to blame others for their mistakes, not only will they not be able to show their skills as a manager, but they might also become the reason for existing staff leaving the company. Bringing a new manager on board has a big impact on existing staff members. Do not just hire them for their past title or past glory—check to see if they are ready to take on a new challenge.

Checkpoints:

- Are they admitting their mistakes?
- Will they cause troubles with their subordinates?
- Are they humble enough to learn from their own mistakes?
- Do they show an eagerness to become one of you?

7 To catch the applicant by surprise

On top of the standard questions, you are sometimes able to get an insight into the applicant's true personality by asking questions the applicant did not expect. Dig in deeper to the answers you are given, and get a glimpse of the applicants' willingness to work and working style.

Which do you think is more important, the content of your job or the labor conditions the job offers?

Most applicants will give job content as the answer. Such applicants may only focus on doing the work they want to do. However, they will be given credit if they fight for better labor conditions through contributing to the company.

What will you do when you disagree with your seniors?

If the applicant simply decides to go with their senior's idea, it shows that you have not earned their trust yet. Subordinates are, of course, expected to listen to their seniors, but they should show their willingness to talk over the issue and be assertive enough to give their seniors their true opinion.

What are your weaknesses at work? (mid-career)

Applicants who are able to self-analyze will be able to tell you their weaknesses, as well as what they are doing about it. If the applicant says they have no weaknesses, they might be telling you what they think you want to hear, or they may be over-confident and self-centered. Over-confident and self-centered people often do not realize they are giving others a hard time, so this may cause trouble with existing staff.

What will you do if you do not receive an offer from our company?

The most common answer you will get is that the applicant will go on applying for jobs in other companies. If the applicant is aiming for the same job type in the same industry, they will be eager to join your company. On the other hand, when you get answers that they have not thought about it yet, you can either take it as a sign that they lack passion or that they have come without a backup plan.

I believe that you may do well in other job types too. What do you think about that? (mid-career)

When the applicant is asked whether they would consider a different job type from the one they have applied for, check their facial expressions as well as their answer. Those who are unhappy about it may not be flexible regarding future job transferals. Those who only care about what they want to do may cause trouble after they join the company. The best answer would be a positive answer of: "If I am capable of doing so."

Is there anyone in this company that you know?

If there is someone they know in the company, ask them about the applicant. Ask about their personality and working ability, if necessary. Dig deeper if such reports have not been documented beforehand.

Checkpoints:

- Are they able to keep calm when they are caught by surprise?
- Are they really eager to join your company?
- Do they show an understanding of your question and give targeted answers?

8 To gain an insight into the applicant's communication skills

To get an insight into the applicant's communication skills, check their way of speaking by engaging the applicant in conversation. If they only get a monosyllabic or overly short response to each question you ask, and have a hard time developing a conversation, the applicant may have poor communication skills. On the other hand, applicants who cannot stop talking and are very self-assertive may fail to read between the lines. This also is a sign of poor communication skills because the applicant lacks the ability to pick up on cues.

Too bad it is raining today.

Start the interview with a conversation about the weather. Applicants who just give a single sentence reply of "Yes, you are right" may have an issue with their communication ability. Check to see if applicants are able to continue the conversation with responses such as, "There hasn't been much rain recently, so at least it will be good for the garden."

By the way, what do you do during your spare time?

This question relates to the applicant's private life, so it should be handled with great care. If you have built a trust relationship with the applicant, go on and ask them this question. If they tell you about sleeping through their holidays or other answers involving no communication with others, you may need to question their communication skills. You can also develop a conversation on the applicant's choice of restaurants by questioning on the topic of food.

How do you deal with people you don't feel comfortable with?

There are all kinds of people working in a company. It is hard to get things done if you cannot work with people you find hard to deal with. Applicants who claim that there are no such people may be avoiding the ones they find difficult to deal with.

Are there things that you bear in mind when talking to your subordinates? (mid-career)

Managers who don't think much about communicating with their subordinates will not be able to build a trust relationship with existing staff. Check on their communication skills by finding out how they have been treating their subordinates in the past. Dig deeper after you get an answer.

Do you communicate much with people outside the company? (mid-career)

Applicants who attend conferences and meetings outside

the company, on top of communicating with their friends and peers, have high communication ability. They should be given credit for jumping into different communities, but do ask about the type of community they are involved in. if the communities are not relevant to their job, you should check on the applicant's personal vision.

Checkpoints:

- Does the conversation develop and continue?
- Do you get a good impression from the applicant's facial expressions and tone when they give an answer?
- Do you find potential for building a good relationship?

9 To gain an insight into the applicant's ability to accommodate

Even the best potential staff will not able to bring their best to work if they lack the ability to accommodate to an organization. In order to get an insight into the applicant's ability to accommodate, you should dig deeper on the questions about communication ability. Applicants who blame their former company and co-workers when talking about their reason for leaving their former company will most likely repeat the same mistakes.

Have you had troubles with human relationships?

You should not take "No" for an answer to this question. Everyone will have experienced such troubles from time to time in their lives. Check if the applicant is able to build good relationships within the organization.

Are there people at work that you dislike?

Check the applicants' facial expressions as they speak about the type of co-workers they dislike. If they are emotional, they may be unable to get work done with such people, thus lacking the ability to accommodate. Check on how they plan to work with the people they dislike.

How do you treat a person when you first meet them?

This question is designed to see if the applicant is conscious about how they build a good relationship with others. Applicants who are self-aware will be able to give solid answers such as listening to others, or greeting them with a smile. However, if the applicant does not have much experience communicating with others, or is not self-aware, they will only be able to give vague answers.

Have you ever worked as part of a team? (mid-career)

Applicants who have mostly worked solo, and have scarce experience of working as part of a team, may find it hard to blend into an organization. If they lack experience, ask them about what they think of teamwork, and check their willingness to work as part of a team.

What is essential to revitalize an organization? (mid-career)

Applicants who have given serious thought to an organization will be able to tell you about their role and what they would do within the organization. If they are only able to give a vague answer, they may lack the imagination to see themselves as part of the organization. Those who only think about themselves will be alienated from other staff.

What do you think of someone younger than you becoming your senior? (mid-career)

This is a question you should ask all applicants who are in the upper years of their life and potentially would end up having a younger staff member as their senior. Most applicants would say that it is not a problem. However, get an insight into how they really see it from their past and from their facial expressions. If they have had a lot of experience in having younger managers, their working ability may be questionable. Make sure they are able to blend in with existing staff.

Checkpoints:

- Are they making an effort to blend in?
- Do they form strong likes and dislikes?
- Do mid-career recruits understand that they are starting to work in a whole new world?

10 To gain an insight into the applicant's sense of responsibility

In relation to students, an insight to an applicant's sense of responsibility can be gained through their extracurricular activities and part-time working experiences. As for mid-career applicants, the same insight can be found from their working experience and their reasons for leaving their prior workplace. Applicants who lack a sense of responsibility blame everyone and everything besides themselves. As long as they work as a professional and are conscious of it, they will be responsible for their own work without giving excuses.

Have you experienced troubles in your extracurricular clubs and activities? (fresh grads)

Check if they are able to reflect calmly on what went wrong and what they could have done better, without blaming anything or anyone. If the applicant has analyzed the issue and learnt from their mistakes, they will be someone to look out for. Those who think they are not to blame will have a high chance of finding history repeating itself.

Can you tell me an episode of failure from your working experience? (mid-career)

Those who claim that they have had no such experiences either do not recognize a failure or think it is not their own failure. You can expect applicants who give an honest answer and are able to tell you how they can use their experience to work responsibly after they join your company.

What is the difference between casual workers and full-time workers? (mid-career)

We are not suggesting that casual workers are not responsible because they are working casually. It is important that casual workers do their work well. On the other hand, full-time workers are responsible for planning and setting-up projects and are the ones who take responsibility for those projects. It is important to check if the applicant is ready to take on responsibility and with a sense of problem solving in mind.

What do you think "responsibility" means when in a work situation? (mid-career)

Those who expect to be paid for their work but refuse to take responsibility for their work are useless to the organization. Make sure the applicant has an awareness of risk and can deal with an impending crisis.

How do you react when things are not going your way? (mid-career)

Applicants who give vague answers such as "It cannot be helped," or say that they will just get over it, may lack a sense of responsibility. The model answer would be to analyze the issue and set solutions to make sure history does not repeat itself.

Checkpoints

- Do they work responsibly?
- Do you see a sense of responsibility from their working experience?
- Are they working with an understanding of their role in your company?

11 To gain an insight into the applicant's stress tolerance

If the applicant has a low tolerance to stress, they will not be able to achieve high after they join the company. They may try to escape difficulties when they arise. It is not only the company that causes stress at work; stress sometimes comes from outside the company. In order to have an insight into the applicants' stress tolerance, a pressure interview can be used. This involves pointing out the things about the applicant that worry you, and observing the facial expressions of the applicant, as well as listening carefully to their responses.

How do you deal with stress?

This is a question aimed at both fresh grads and mid-career applicants. The question is about how the applicant sees stress. You should be doubtful about every other answer you receive if an applicant answers this one by saying that they do not feel stress. If an applicant already has a strategy to tackle stress, they will be able to use it after joining your company.

How do you change your mood when things are not going as planned? (mid-career)

Applicants who know how to deal with stress will be able to change their mood without getting stressed out. Check not only the ways the applicant changes their mood, but also check if they identify and deal with the roots of the issue as well.

It seems that you have only been talking about your part-time working experience—what about your studies? (fresh grads)

Honest applicants will willingly admit their fault in not referring to their studies. You can be sure that applicants who give excuses to everything will do the same after joining the company.

You have been changing jobs very frequently—are you going to change jobs soon this time as well? (mid-career pressure interview)

Use a strong tone as you ask this question. A pressure interview is never on the top of the list of the to-dos. However, when applicants fail to tell you what they really think, ask with a pressuring tone, and observe not only their answer but also their facial expressions. If they seem to have complaints, they may end up getting into trouble with human relationships in and out of the company.

The blank period since you left your last workplace has been long—are you sure you are still capable of working? (mid-career pressure interview)

It takes time to get back on track after a long leave. This question gives you an insight into the applicant's eagerness to start work again. Dig in deeper if the blank period was not used on something related to the job such as further study.

Checkpoints:

- Do they know how to deal with stress?
- Do they have a rebellious expression when their faults are presented to them?
- Can they admit their faults and humbly reflect on what they can do to improve?

12 To gain an insight into the applicant's enthusiasm for a new field

Fresh grads will have had no working experience in any field besides what they have done in a part-time job. Therefore, their enthusiasm towards the job can be observed through their intentions and self-evaluation. On the other hand, there are mid-career applicants who change jobs, and even job types, whenever they find themselves hating what they are doing. Therefore, you need to see what they really think of the job. Applicants for mid-career positions are expected to become part of the workforce quickly. They will not be able to do this if they have not been enthusiastic enough to study for the required skills and knowledge in their own time. Make sure you see how earnest the applicant is when they apply for a job they are inexperienced in.

Have you ever done any self-development training?

For example, if the job requires language skills, applicants are expected to give an answer about current self-study to improve their skills. This question gives an insight into the efforts the applicant has made to get an offer from the company.

Why are you applying for a job in a new field where you have no experience? (mid-career)

If the applicant can only give a vague answer to the reason for applying for a job type they are not experienced in, they may be trying to escape from what they have been doing before. For mid-career applicants, no one will be treating them as newbies even though they may not be experienced, thus they should not become part of the workforce unless they are really willing to learn.

Are you okay with young supervisors? (mid-career)

Mid-career applicants who lack experience will require supervisors after they enter the company. Observe not only their answer to this question, but also their facial expressions and attitude. If they are serious about becoming part of the workforce, they will have a calm expression and not be bothered by the age of their supervisor.

Your wages will be much less than what you have been getting—are you fine with that? (mid-career)

It is only natural for the wages to start low when a worker is inexperienced. However, there are some applicants who hope for the same wage because they have the same financial commitments. Applicants who are not aware that they are inexperienced will have no room for growth.

Tell me about your vision for the future. (mid-career)

Depending on the type of job, some mid-career applicants apply for a job type where they have no experience with the aim of learning the know-hows on the job and through self-development in their own time. Ask not only for the reason they are applying for a job in a field where they have no experience, but also check if your company has what it takes to make the applicant's vision come true.

Checkpoints:

- Do they understand what they need to do? Or are they just dreaming about the job?
- Is the applicant changing jobs because they hate their former job?
- Are they working in their own time for self-development?

13 Questions one hesitates to ask

You cannot ask about an applicant's private life during an interview, but some HR personnel still worry that single applicants may get married and quit the job in the near future. It is also necessary to double-check if the applicant has the understanding and support of their partner and extended family. You should not ask direct questions about marriage and child rearing. However, it is possible to ask such questions by twisting them a little once a trust relation has been established. Make sure that you do not make the applicant feel uneasy as you ask the questions.

What do you think about working in the future? (mid-career)

Although the applicant may realize they are really being asked about marriage and child rearing, they are able to give an answer without feeling uneasy because it was not asked directly. Observe female applicants' facial expressions to see how earnest they are as they claim that they would continue working even after marriage.

What would you do if your partner were transferred to a different workplace? (mid-career)

This question gives you an insight into whether the applicant has their partner's support. It is a hard question, but most applicants when applying for a full-time job answer that they would be prepared to work away from their family when necessary. If the applicant looks away as they speak, they may not mean what they say.

What would you do if your child were to fall sick? (mid-career)

Depending on the type of job, it is difficult to give an offer without the support of the applicant's partner and extended family. If they are able to give a solid answer to what they would do if their child fell sick, the applicant definitely has a strong eagerness to work. However, if the applicant shows hesitation, they may struggle to get help from their family.

Can you balance work and life? (mid-career)

Applicants who simply say "Yes" without any specific plans may not have thought about it deeply enough. Applicants who are eager to get the job will offer details about how they will balance work and life, such as through the support of their partner and family. When you get a very simple answer, try to ask the applicant what her partner does. Observe their facial expressions as well as their answers.

Are you okay with overnight business trips?

If it is impossible for family reasons, the applicant should make it clear beforehand. It may develop into a larger problem if you fail to double-check with the applicant during an interview before they join the company.

Checkpoints:

- Do not ask anything that would make the applicant feel uncomfortable
- Build a trust relationship and ask according to the job content
- Ask about worrying factors during the interview

14 Insights from questions the applicant asks

By now, you should be able to build a picture of the applicant's personality by their responses to your questions. If the applicant asks about something that has already been explained, their ability to understand or to listen may be questionable. If an applicant asks about the labor conditions and wages, they may fail to stay with the company unless they are satisfied with the conditions. Applicants who are eager to work will be asking about the content of the job and what they will be expected to do.

[Applicants asking multiple questions]

When an applicant bombards the interviewer with questions, they may lack an understanding of the interviewing situation. There are applicants who try to show their passion by asking multiple questions. On the other hand, there are also applicants who repeat the same questions in the hope of finding their dream company. Such applicants only think of themselves and do not think about what contributions they can make.

[Applicants who fixate on labor conditions]

Suitable applicants will ask about what they would be

doing if they get the job, not about the conditions. Those who ask only about the wages and holidays may jump into another company if the conditions there are better than yours. Those who are insistent about their starting wage lack confidence, and do not expect to be promoted. However, the starting wage is a legitimate concern, so please give a clear explanation.

[Applicants asking about introductory training]

Fresh grads have no working experience, thus you cannot blame them for asking about training. However, if a mid-career applicant is fixated on the introductory training system of the company, they may be passive workers, and they may not become part of the workforce quickly enough. It is important that they show an eagerness to improve their skills. However, it is hard to accept an application from applicants who appear to only care about their own career upgrades or promotions.

[Applicants asking about the company's achievements]

Applicants can research the achievements of the company for themselves. Therefore, applicants that ask such questions are either those who have not done thorough research on the company, or applicants who are aiming for stability. If a fresh grad applicant asks such questions, despite the fact that it has been explained during information sessions, question their ability to listen or understand. Applicants who understand that the company's achievements are built on experience and are determined to help it grow even more are the applicants you are after.

[Applicants asking about transferals between departments and workplaces]

Applicants asking about transferals between departments and workplaces are usually those who do not want to be transferred. Even if they say they do not mind, they nonetheless want to know what really happens. If there is a possibility of a transferal, make sure you explain it honestly and in detail.

Checkpoints:

- Are they insistent about conditions?
- Are their questions caused by concern?
- Are they prioritizing how they can contribute to the company?

Column 6

Bring existing staff into the picture

If you are conducting an interview for a specific department, ask staff from that department to sit in the interview with you. Similar to the company information session, it is important to pull other staff other than the HR crew into the picture. If the department refuses, citing a busy workload, they should think twice. No company can run without its people. Companies in which the managers lead the recruiting of new staff are companies that cherish their staff. Such managers take a hands-on role in the organization, strongly influencing its culture.

Most job hunters worry about whether they will get along with the existing staff of the company, and if they will be able to blend into the new workplace. To show that the whole company welcomes new staff, you should involve current staff in the recruitment process. Don't forget, not all applicants have put your company as their first choice: good workers are on the look out for the right company.

CHAPTER 7

PREVENT YOUR UNOFFICIAL OFFER BEING DECLINED

When, after all your hard work, you make an applicant an unofficial offer and they turn it down, you might think that you have wasted your time and money. You might just give up on those who do not seem to want to work in your company. However, it is important to understand the psychology of the prospective employee and make necessary follow-ups after giving them an unofficial offer.

When prospective employees decline their offer, most of them end up swaying between emotions and wanting the job back. Do not go after them. Rather, put your efforts into predicting their actions before they decline the offer, and give them the follow-up they need.

1 Understand the applicant's psychology

The applicant would have been giving all they had before they received the unofficial offer, but once they get the offer, they start to worry about whether this is the company for them. If the applicant has an existing job, they will need to resign their job. Their current employer might ask them to think twice about their decision.

In fresh graduate recruitment, it is common for prospective employees to apply for other companies because they still have time up their sleeve. But older prospective employees are expected to enter the company within a few months, which gives them not much time to decide if they should accept the offer or not.

The person in charge of recruitment, who was probably warm and helpful during the recruitment process, may now become busy and hard to reach. Even if the prospective employee does make contact, this person can seem distant and indifferent.

If you think that a prospective employee will join your company simply by giving them an offer, you are being shortsighted because there is nothing to prevent them declining your offer. The prospective employee has only the person in charge to count on. **If they feel that this person is unfriendly, they may decline their offer and think badly of the company.** As for prospective employees who currently have a job, they may think that there are other companies, or even their current company, that suit them better.

Do not just rely on e-mails and phone calls. Make an effort to ask the prospective employee to visit the company, and hand them their contract in person. By giving them a written contract, both parties will be bound legally. However, there are companies that do not give the prospective employee a contract because they want to decide on the exact workplace location and working conditions after the prospective employee joins the company. Please understand that the prospective employee rarely demands a written contract, even if it's what they want.

The prospective employee's emotions will be all over the place from the time they receive an offer till they join the company. Thus you must follow-up on them and let them know that you are still there for them. Consider the time and expense you have spent finding your prospective employee— don't let them slip away now.

Prospective employees will be wondering if they have made the right choice. To help them reach a decision, a friendly hand from the person who has recruited them may be all that's needed.

Remember, your work continues until the people you have recruited become part of the workforce and start benefiting the company. Become a HR person who can think from the prospective employee's shoes.

The applicant's psychology after receiving an unofficial offer:

- Unsure if they have made the right choice
- Not sure if there are companies more suitable for them out there
- Put off by the apparently indifferent attitude of the person who has recruited them

2 Check for falsehoods during the adoption stage

To prevent successful applicants from declining an unofficial offer, you should check on their documents during the adoption stage while proceeding with the official procedures. The letter of acceptance of a job offer is standard practice for fresh grads, but some companies leave it out for mid-career recruits because of the short period between giving an offer and having them join the company.

By setting a deadline for sending in the letter of acceptance of a job offer, you will be able to assess the applicant's eagerness to join your company. If the deadline for a reply is set within a week, you will still have time (if your first choice declines the offer) to whip up some new offers to applicants whom you have kept on hold. Always have a backup plan.

In the letter of acceptance of a job offer, add in a point that the offer may be cancelled or the applicant may be dismissed if there are falsehoods in their documents. By doing so, you will be able to sieve out the applicants who hand in fake documents. Applicants who hand in documents with falsehoods will not become good workers. Therefore, it is very important to check properly before they join the company.

There are prospective employees who fail to hand in their identification papers. Make sure you ask for their reason. Those who are unable to present their identification papers for personal issues may have something hidden in their past that has not been checked during the recruitment period. Talk to them in person. There are also cases where the prospective employee may be having trouble finding a personal referee. The company should have plans on what to do in these cases as well.

The statement of earnings is usually handed in around the end of the year. Check if the statement corresponds with what the new employee stated during the recruitment period. If they have been laid off, their actual earnings will be less than what they have stated. Of course, nobody will be fired just because they haven't stated that they were laid off during the time of recruitment. However, it is necessary to speak to the new employee and ask for the details. If the new employees figure that your check system is lenient and easy to get through, be prepared for future trouble from sloppy working attitudes.

In the case of mid-career recruitments, many companies choose not to ask for the applicant's graduation certificate. However, what is written on the résumé is not always accurate. By asking for the prospective employees' graduate certificates, the credibility of the prospective employee's academic history will be assured. Although it is understandable that you will not want to cancel the offers you have given, **employees that have entered the company on a lie will tend to look down on the management system of the company. It will increase the risk of history repeating itself.** So if you detect a lie, consider cancelling the job offer.

Check for falsehoods during the adoption stages:

- Attach a document in regard to faulty information to the letter of acceptance of job offer
- Ask for the prospective employee's identification papers
- Double-check the prospective employee's statement of earnings
- Make sure you get all applicants' graduate certificates, including mid-career applicants

3 Follow-up applicants who are given an unofficial offer (fresh grads)

When recruiting for fresh graduates, there is a gap between their offer and their entry to the company. Therefore, following-up applicants who are given an unofficial offer is very important. At orientation and training, it is crucial for prospective employees to fit into the working mode and network between themselves.

Training for prospective employees before they join the company should be at the right level for a student, including educational games and content that will improve the prospective employees' understanding of the company. Think about it more as an opportunity to network with your future staff and for them to network with each other.

Holding training sessions frequently may not be advisable because students may not be able to attend because of academic commitments. Once every three months is about right. After a few hours of training, hold a social gathering for them just to socialize. Through socializing and talking to senior staff, you will be able to take the stress off prospective employees' shoulders.

Besides training, ask prospective employees to send you an e-mail or report every month on how they are feeling. You will be able to tell if the prospective employee needs help by reading what they write, including between the lines. You can then give a follow-up when needed.

The condition of prospective employees can be determined not only by the content of the e-mail, but also by the word count. If you get an extremely short e-mail, the prospective employee may be comparing you with other companies. Contact them before they call in to turn down their offer, and give them a hand if they need any help.

If your company is holding a social event or management strategy briefing, invite as many prospective employees as you can and introduce them to your current staff. By doing so, the prospective employees will get the impression that they are already part of the company. However, prospective employees have not entered the company yet, so make attendance optional.

Another way to build a network between you and prospective employees is through SNS sites. Through communicating on SNS websites, you can let the prospective employees be at ease and they can build up a network of their own. However, networking in an environment with prospective employees only may lead to confusion of what is going on. So include a human resources staff member in the group and keep them updated on the company's information.

In order to prevent prospective employees declining their offers, it is important to give them the impression that they are in the same boat with the other staff. By building a linkage between the prospective employees and the company, the prospective employees will be able to join the company already in a working mode.

Follow-ups for applicants who are given an unofficial offer (fresh grads):

- Build a connection with prospective employees through prospective employee training
- Ask the prospective employees for regular reports on how they have been
- Use SNS tools to network with the prospective employees
- Do not go after prospective employees who have declined your offer—predict their behavior instead

4   Follow-up applicants who are given an unofficial offer (mid-career recruits)

When recruiting mid-career, the gap until the prospective employees enter the company tends to be very short, yet long enough for a prospective employee to decline the offer. Stop thinking that everyone will jump right in once they receive an offer. Do your best to follow-up on the prospective employees to ease their worries and concerns.

Some prospective employees become unsure if this is the company they want to enter after they receive the offer. If the follow-up is not impressive, they might treat that as one of their reasons for declining the offer.

Because of the short gap, many companies tend to get things done simply and quickly through paperwork and over the phone. But you should try to arrange a time for the prospective employees to come to the company and let them speak to their future colleagues. **They may be fretting about whether they will be able to get along with the existing staff. Simply by meeting with the existing staff, they will be able to get an image of what they are expected to do at work, and will ultimately join the company with some understanding of their work.**

If the prospective employees find the current staff warm and welcoming, they will feel less nervous and worried as they make the final decision to join the company.

If a prospective employee needs a few months to get out of their prior job, ask them to give you regular updates, even if it is just a monthly thing. Worthy employees are usually pursued to stay when they attempt to leave. The prospective employees might feel confused. If they fail to receive any contact from your company, they may choose to stay in the company they are working for.

There are cases of prospective employees negotiating a higher pay, despite the former agreement on their entry wages. Generally, you should not be changing the agreed wage. There is a high chance that the applicants who fixate on their pay will ask for the same favor a few months after you give in and change their wage. Tell them what they should do to earn an increase in wage; get them to earn it for themselves. If the applicants are not happy with this decision, you might have to consider taking back your offer, given that you need to ensure there is a right balance between new and existing staff in regard to pay and conditions.

Unlike fresh graduate recruits, the entry period varies for mid-career recruits. Get their nametags, business cards and knick-knacks ready by the time they arrive. This will make the new staff feel welcomed and enhance their motivation.

Approach your prospective employees warmly, thanking them for choosing your company over other companies. The HR personnel are the only people the prospective employees are able to get in touch with. Do not leave the follow-ups to the front desk. Show prospective employees that you care and are interested in them.

Follow-up care for prospective employees is an important part of recruitment.

Follow-ups for applicants who are given an unofficial offer (mid-career):

- The HR crew should follow-up the applicant even after the applicant receives an offer
- Ask the prospective employee to come to the company for follow-up care, if necessary
- Keep in touch during the gap period before they join the company
- Introduce the prospective employee to the existing staff

Column 7

Think about what to do when the applicant declines your offer

When someone declines the offer you have made them, you may feel angry or at least have mixed feelings. I used to get upset when I received such information, exclaiming: "What are they thinking!" and "What a waste of time!" I used to think that it was the applicant who was at fault, and did not think about the reasons behind them deciding not to join the company.

There is no point in thinking badly of the applicant. I should have started reflecting on whether I had done enough follow up. Perhaps I had looked down on them during an interview, thus making it easier for our company to be outbid by another company. Both the company and the applicant have the right to choose. Although it is shame that you are losing your potential staff, moaning about it does not change a thing. When many people decline your company's offer, you should think in their shoes, and reflect on the reasons that caused them to make the decision.

CHAPTER 8

CARE FOR YOUR NEW STAFF

Fresh grads and mid-career applicants alike will feel at sea when they first come to your company. Remember, your job is not finished until they are fully integrated into your workforce and feel that they "fit in".

1 Setting in the fresh grad recruits

In order to settle fresh grads that have no full-time working experience, one year of attentive care is necessary. Do not think that you can just leave it to their assigned department. Make the effort to create a system for the fresh grads to stay in your company worry-free.

[Introduce a brother-and-sister system]

One of the ways to settle fresh grads is to ask a senior employee of the same age group to take care of them as their "brother" or "sister." This is also known in some workplaces as the "buddy system." The same age group is important because, in the new grad's eyes, their superior may be hard to approach because of the age gap. Similarly, the superior may find the fresh grad's problems hard to understand because of their difference in age.

The "brother" or "sister" will supervise the fresh grads' daily work, giving them advice and instructions. When the fresh grad encounters a problem, they will have someone approachable to turn to.

Through introducing a brother-and-sister system, the young senior employee will develop a consciousness to guide their juniors. They are also able to think in the fresh grad's shoes and give appropriate advice, as both of them will be close in age.

Before the newly hired is assigned to a department, gather the "brothers" and "sisters" who are going to take care of the newly hired and explain to them the purpose of the brother-and-sister system. If the system is criticized within the company, the newly hired will be affected. Therefore, it is crucial to pay attention to not only the newly hired but also their seniors. Do not just praise the new recruits' efforts to fit in, but also give credit to the senior staff looking after them.

When troubles occur with the newly hired, there may be issues that the brother-and sister-system cannot deal with. Make sure these problems are reported to superiors.

[Setting in the mid-career recruits]

For mid-career recruitments, it is not necessary to place them in the brother-and-sister system. However, they will be just as unfamiliar with your company as the fresh graduates. Make sure they have a supervisor they can turn to when they are unsure of anything.

For the first three months, the newly hired tend to be

overwhelmed by all the new things they are experiencing. Mid-career recruits may compare your company to their former workplace, regretting their decision to come over. Even experienced workers will feel uneasy in a totally new environment. Things will be worse if they do not get along with the existing staff. The newly hired may end up thinking that your company is not the place for them

By setting up a system to take away the newly hired employees' worries and letting their voice be heard, the stability of the workforce will be assured and you will have not wasted your efforts in recruiting them.

Introduce a brother-and-sister system:

- Let the seniors take care of the juniors
- Report to superiors when there is a problem with a newly hired employee
- Give credit to the brother-and-sister system
- Cast a supervisor for the newly hired mid-career employee to lean on

2 Ask new staff to hand in a monthly report to HR

The best way to know how the newly hired employee is faring in their assigned department is to have them give you a monthly report. Otherwise, all you will know about them will come from their superiors. If they are not getting along well with their superiors, they may be reported as useless. You cannot exclude the possibility that the problem lies with the superior. Therefore, you should not just hear the story from one side, but from both sides in order to know how the newly hired employee is really doing. There are also cases of newly hired employees rebelliously disobeying orders from their superiors because they are discontented with their superiors' way of handling issues.

In the report, ask the newly hired to write about the tasks they are working on, things that they want to work on, the problems they are facing, and how to overcome them. When newly hired employees start off reporting well but then start to have problems in meeting the deadline or their reports start to lack content, you might need to set up a consulting session to find out the reasons.

Through understanding the current work progress and

the troubles the newly hired are facing, the HR crew is able to talk to their superiors about it, or even handle the report as a company issue.

Even though the superiors and HR would be telling the newly hired to 'Come to me anytime', try to understand that it is not such an easy thing for a newbie to seek help. Fresh grads are new to the company and lack full-time working experience. They tend to find the apples on the other side of the fence sweeter. They may even develop a wrong mindset for working through their problems by talking to their other working friends.

The reports should continue for at least one year. You will then be able to tell how much the new employee has grown. One thing you have to bear in mind is that if you fail to handle the newly hired employee's problems, they will lose trust in you. Make sure that you follow-up on what is written in the report. By doing so, they will feel looked after, leading to honest reports.

After recruiting for one year and assigning the newly hired to their departments, it will be time to start planning for the following year's recruitment. It may be tough, but do not slack off caring for the newly hired staff while you start the process for attracting a fresh round of recruits.

Every worker has been new to an organization at least once. It is easy to forget how it felt like to be new to a place once you have been there for a long time. But keep this in mind: **companies that understand and care for their new staff are those that grow.**

Ask them to hand in a report monthly to HR:

- Ask the newly hired to hand in a monthly report to HR
- Handle problems stated in the report immediately
- Keep track of what the newly hired employee is working on
- Keep in mind that attentive care leads to growth

3 Make full use of the career sheet

As new employees that are fresh from university have no practical working experience, they are often lost and unsure of what they should be doing. Their seniors and superiors may expect them to watch and learn, but it may be hard for some newly hired employees to catch on. In order for them to understand what they should be doing, the career sheet should be put into full use.

What should be done is stated specifically on the career sheet. As it is all in black and white, the newly hired employee should be able to understand their individual progress.

After they have been in the company for a certain period of time, ask them to use the career sheet (see Chapter 9 for a template) to check the tasks they are capable of doing. The tasks will differ for different work fields. Next, ask their superiors to check on their practical skills, referring to the career sheet.

There will be times when the superior will think the new employee is still incapable of doing some tasks that the new employee thinks themselves fully capable of doing, and vice versa. Through using the career sheet, an interview may be conducted to explain the superior's evaluation. Focus on the points that do not agree and look for the reasons for this.

The superiors will find it easier to explain working tasks when there are specific guidelines to check against. The newly hired employee will also find specific comments acceptable. These are the merits of using a career sheet. **Through giving new employees a chance to sit down and talk to their superiors, a good relationship can be built.**

There are things that should be pointed out on the spot. However, superiors giving comments on the career sheet will not only help improve the working skills of the new employee, but also let them feel that their work is actually being seen and acknowledged.

Career sheets are different from HR feedback interviews. The latter are filled with vague content and even run the risk of destroying the relationship built between the newly hired employee and their superior. In contrast, career sheets are based on practical work. Through ticking the boxes of what the newly hired should do, their working skills and motivation will increase.

Even for mid-career recruitments with little prior experience, you can expect them to become powerful workers in a short period through putting the career sheet to work.

Make full use of the career sheet:

- Understand the newly hired employee's level of working ability
- Know the points of disagreement in an evaluation between the newly hired employee and their superior
- Build up a trust relationship through specific observations and advice
- Help the newly hired employee see their improvements with their own eyes

CHAPTER 9

HELPFUL
DOCUMENTS

The current status check

- -

1 = Yes   2 = Neither   3 = No

Business management	Check		
1. The company has a strong position in the industry for its goods and services.	1.	2.	3.
2. Marketing policies are clear and supported by staff.	1.	2.	3.
3. No deficits have been accumulating for the last 5 years.	1.	2.	3.
4. Ordinary profit has been increasing each year.	1.	2.	3.
5. "Thank-you parties"' and AGMs are carried out.	1.	2.	3.
Working environment	Check		
6. The workplace is within 10 minutes' walk from public transport.	1.	2.	3.
7. Computers are all set up.	1.	2.	3.
8. Male and female washrooms are separated.	1.	2.	3.
9. The average age of the staff is under 35.	1.	2.	3.
10. Ten percent or less newly hired resign from their job within their first 3 years in the company.	1.	2.	3.

11. Office regulations, wage regulations, and retirement allowance regulations are open for regular staff to read.	1. 2. 3.
12. Directions and command systems are set up.	1. 2. 3.
Career plan	**Check**
13. The HR department gives feedback to you.	1. 2. 3.
14. There are a lot of projects suggested and run by staff under the age of 25.	1. 2. 3.
15. The career path is clear.	1. 2. 3.
16. The company recruits continuously for fresh grads, and there are no big changes in the number of offers sent out.	1. 2. 3.
17. More than 20% of the staff is under 30 years of age.	1. 2. 3.
Labor conditions, wages	**Check**
18. Overtime is paid.	1. 2. 3.
19. OT hours are under 30 hours per month.	1. 2. 3.
20. Working hours are under 40 hours per week (excluding OT hours).	1. 2. 3.

The current status check

- -

1 = Yes   2 = Neither   3 = No

21. More than 20% of employees earn more than 5 million yen per year.	1. 2. 3.
22. The company has not received warnings from the Labor Standards Inspection Office for the last 3 years.	1. 2. 3.
23. There are employees that are either taking maternity leave or nursing leave.	1. 2. 3.

Total   ( ) ( ) ( )

Checkpoints during an interview

	Checkpoints	Check
First impressions	Calm and able to greet warmly.	
	Good eye contact with the interviewer.	
	Smiling, giving a good impression.	
	Neat and tidy outfit and hairstyle.	
Intentions of entry	Prioritizing your company as their first choice.	
	Application based on the understanding of their aptitudes and strengths.	
	Able to talk about what they are able to do for (or want to do in) your company.	
	Have a concrete career plan for working in your company.	
Working ability and aptitude	Able to utilize their knowledge and aptitude (fresh grads).	
	Able to utilize experience, thus potentially part of the workforce in a short period (mid-career).	
	Able to utilize working experience despite being inexperienced in their current field (mid-career).	

	Checkpoints	Check
Reasons for leaving their previous job (mid-career)	Credible experience and achievements.	
	They have a plan that is achievable in your company.	
	They see negatives as opportunities.	
	Chances are low that history will repeat itself in your company.	
	In case of leaving due to illness or health issues, it does not affect them working now.	
	It is not the applicant to blame if they were fired.	
	Their reasons for leaving their current company and their intentions of joining your company are related.	
	They understand that they have a blank period after quitting their job.	
Personality	They appear to really listen.	
	They understand and react correctly to the conversation.	

Checkpoints during an interview

	Checkpoints	Check
	They are able to work well with existing staff.	
	They are positive about things.	
	They are bright and confident.	
	Their speech is credible and trustworthy.	
	They are able to read between the lines and care for their surroundings.	
	They have not lost confidence in themselves.	
	They have no financial issues.	
	They appear to have a calm personality.	
	They are healthy and do not have any family issues.	

Interview checklist (fresh grads)

1 = Bad   2 = Average   3 = Good

Entering the room — sitting down	Check
Has a good understanding of business manners, such as knocking on the door.	1. 2. 3.
Greets nicely on entering the room.	1. 2. 3.
Dressed neatly and gives a good impression.	1. 2. 3.
About their school/university life	**Check**
Attended with an aim.	1. 2. 3.
Has experience in working part-time or their major study area can be utilized to benefit the company.	1. 2. 3.
Has good academic results.	1. 2. 3.
Has played a leading role in extracurricular activities or similar.	1. 2. 3.
Intention of entry	**Check**
There is a relation to their experience.	1. 2. 3.
Knows the company well.	1. 2. 3.
Has a vision about their future career.	1. 2. 3.
Can give a solid speech on why they have applied for the position.	1. 2. 3.

Date: _____

- -

Name of applicant: _____

Name of interviewer: _____

Self-appeal of applicants	Check
Able to talk about how their strengths and skills will benefit the company.	1. 2. 3.
Understands their strengths.	1. 2. 3.
Communication skills	**Check**
Easy to understand and speaks clearly.	1. 2. 3.
Able to give a good impression through a conversation.	1. 2. 3.
Understands instructions.	1. 2. 3.
After the interview	**Check**
Shows a strong eagerness to work in the company.	1. 2. 3.

Travelling time to work	
1. Needs to move house 2. 1–2 hours traffic 3. Within 1 hour	Ways to travel to work [ ]

Family is	
1. Problematic 2. Average 3. Supportive	Situation in applications to other companies [ ]

Interviewer's notes:

Interview checklist (mid-career)

1 = Bad   2 = Average   3 = Good

Entering the room — sitting down	Check
Has a good understanding of business manners, such as knocking on the door.	1. 2. 3.
Greets warmly as they enter the room.	1. 2. 3.
Dressed neatly and gives a good impression.	1. 2. 3.
About their previous work experience	Check
Able to give examples and remarks to support their explanations.	1. 2. 3.
Answers are concrete and credible.	1. 2. 3.
Has the ability and working experience that can be utilized to benefit the company.	1. 2. 3.
Can benefit the company even if the field is not familiar to them.	1. 2. 3.
Reason for leaving	Check
Has a good reason—not escaping from reality.	1. 2. 3.
Intentions of entry	Check
There is a relation to their experience.	1. 2. 3.
Wishes to achieve something in the company that they could not do in their former workplace.	1. 2. 3.

Date: _____

- -

Name of applicant: _____

Name of interviewer: _____

Able to give a solid reason for their application.	1. 2. 3.
Self-appeal of applicants	Check
Able to talk about how their strengths and skills will benefit the company.	1. 2. 3.
Self-evaluation of applicants	Check
Able to talk about their strengths based on their experience.	1. 2. 3.
Understands their strengths.	1. 2. 3.
Communication skills	Check
Easy to understand and speaks clearly.	1. 2. 3.
Able to give a good impression through conversation.	1. 2. 3.
Understands instructions.	1. 2. 3.
After the interview	Check
Shows a strong eagerness to work in the company.	1. 2. 3.
Travelling time to work	
1. Needs to move house 2. 1–2 hours traffic 3. Within 1 hour	Ways to travel to work [ ]

Interview checklist (mid-career)

- -

Family is
1. Problematic
2. Average
3. Supportive

Time needed before they can enter the company	
1. More than 4 months	Desired wages
2. 1–3 months	
3. Less than 1 month	[ ]

Interviewer's notes:

Career sheet (customer service)

- -

1 = Bad   2 = Average   3 = Good

Goal for 3 months' time (Dated:_____)
(   )

Accomplishment of goal (Dated:_____)
(   )

Tick the boxes of accomplishment, and put an X in boxes of items that the employee is not capable of doing. Hand in to superior after the employee fills in the form.

	Date:		
Items	Employee	Superior	
Serves customers with a smile.			
Able to greet people and leave a good impression.			
Speaks in an appropriate tone.			
Does not show tiredness through facial expressions or attitudes.			
Remembers customers' names.			
Hairstyle and outfit are neat and clean.			
Works well in a team.			
Serves customers appropriately according to the situation.			
Able to handle complaints.			
Able to attract fixed customers.			

Date: _____

- -

Name (Employee): _____

Name (Superior): _____

Goal for 6 months' time (Dated:_____)
(   )

Accomplishment of goal (Dated:_____)
(   )

Date:		Comments
Employee	Superior	

Career sheet (customer service)

	Date:		
Items	Employee	Superior	
Able to write a daily report.			
Can problem-solve.			
Earns praise from customers.			
Able to arrange work shifts.			
Able to give guidance to part-time workers.			
Able to give advice on selling products.			

	Date:		Comments
	Employee	Superior	

Questions in the book

○ for a good answer   ✕ for a bad answer

[Questions applying Maslow's law]

What is your motivation for going to work?

○ Gives an answer about what motivates them to go to work and what their priorities are

✕ Gives a vague answer

Have you gained experienced from failures?

○ Talks about the lessons learnt through failure

✕ Had no episodes to share, thus gives a vague answer

What do you see as self-fulfillment?

○ Has a clear direction

✕ Gives a vague answer with no clear direction

[Questions to check on EQ]

Please tell me specifically what you have learnt from a past failure.

○ Perceives a past failure as a lesson for the future

✕ Seems to have leant nothing from past mistakes; has a low consciousness of failure

Have you achieved anything as part of a team?

○ Talks about their experiences of working as part of a team

✕ Has no episodes of working as a team to share

Are you able to control your emotions when things aren't going well?

○ Is calm and able to control their emotions

✕ Is not conscious of such problems, or not able to control their emotions

How do you accommodate others?

○ Is conscious about the need to accommodate others and gives a solid answer

✕ Does not appear to be conscious of the need to accommodate others

Standard questions

[Follow-up questions on the reason for applying]

What is the career goal you wish to achieve?

○ Has a goal that can be fulfilled in your company

✕ Gives a vague answer that could be achieved anywhere

What can you only achieve in our company?

○ Talks about the special features of the company, showing their eagerness to join

✕ Stays silent, not able to give a concrete reason

What do you think you should do to achieve your goals?

○ Gives a solid answer related to the job requirements of the position

✕ Has no idea, thus gives a vague answer

How did you research our company?

○ Researched through different media

✕ Only read the recruitment ad and the company's homepage

[Follow-up questions on self-evaluation]

Give some specific examples.

○ Gives specific examples of job experiences that can be utilized

✕ Only gives vague answers that cannot be utilized

How are you able to leverage in our company?

○ Gives an answer related to the recruiting position

✕ Gives a vague answer—unable to leverage in the company

What did others say about your ability?

○ Gives remarks from a third party relevant to the job

✕ Gives a vague answer irrelevant to the job

Give me a self-evaluation of something other than your school or academic life.

○ Reacts calmly, giving a self-evaluation based on working experience

✕ Panics and is unsure of what to say

Standard questions

[Questions that branch from the strengths and weaknesses]

Give an example from your experience that explains your strengths.

○ Describes episodes that can be leveraged into their jobs
✕ Fails to give anything but a vague answer

How would you put your strengths to work in our company?

○ Paints a picture of themselves actively working
✕ Gives a vague answer; hard to picture them as a worker

Have your weaknesses ever affected your work?

○ No, or being able to resolve the problem when issues arise
✕ May cause trouble after joining the company

Are you trying to overcome your weaknesses?

○ Gives specific ideas for overcoming their weaknesses
✕ Does not give specific ideas for solving any problems

[Questions that branch from their school or academic life (fresh grads)]

How would you make the best of your experience?

○ Gives a concrete answer based on their understanding of the job

✕ Unable to give an answer, or gives a vague answer

Did you experience problems related to personal relationships during club activities?

○ Have learnt lessons, and explains how they would solve the problem

✕ Unable to answer due to a lack of consciousness about relationships

What from your casual work experience can you leverage into work?

○ Gives a solid answer and paints a bright and lively picture

✕ Unable to answer due to lack of research

Are you not interested in the field you have worked casually for?

○ Talks about the industry your company is in with a passion

✕ Looks lost

Standard questions

[Questions that branch from their job history (mid-career)]

Give me specific examples of something you have achieved.

○ Gives an impression that they have high working ability

✕ Unable to form an image of applicant's achievements because of their vague answer

We have a unique working style. Are you okay with that?

○ Shows an eagerness to fit in

✕ Looks worried

Is it fine that we are in a different working field?

○ Looks confident because they have thoroughly researched the industry

✕ Unsure due to lack of research

Do you have any management experience?

○ Gives specific examples

✕ Unable to provide an example or seems uninterested

[Questions that branch from their reasons for leaving (mid-career)]

Will you leave our company for the same reason?

○ Shows an eagerness to join your company and not any other

✕ Shows no evidence that they would stay

I don't seem to read a flow in your past jobs.

○ Accepts the fact and gives a solid explanation

✕ Unable to give a clear explanation

Were you unable to do what you wanted to do in your former workplace?

○ Gives a solid explanation of why they were unable to do so

✕ Reason given lacks credibility

Why are you changing jobs in the same work field?

○ Links up their answer with their intentions of entry, giving a positive response

✕ Gives a vague answer that lacks credibility

Standard questions

[A twist on reasons for applying]

Why us out of all the other companies out there?

○ Describes the specific aspects that your company has that differ from any other

✕ Gives a vague answer that could be applied to any company

Why did you apply to us, a company that is in the same field as your former company? (mid-career)

○ Shows what they are capable of doing without denying their former workplace

✕ Shows confusion and unable to give a clear answer

Are you applying for companies offering similar jobs?

○ Shows their beliefs and passion about the industry

✕ Gives a vague answer that includes a description of other industries

[A twist on self-evaluation]

Give me a self-evaluation of what you could do only in our company.

○ Able to give a solid answer on their strengths and why they are able to leverage in your company

✕ Gives a vague answer—unable to picture what they can do

Try to promote yourself as if you are a product for sale.

○ Understands the question and gives an appropriate pitch

✕ Misunderstands the question and fails to respond appropriately

Give me an example of a strength you can leverage in our company.

○ Immediately nominates a required ability as one of their strengths

✕ Unable to filter down to a single answer

Standard questions

[A twist on job history (or school/academic life)]

Tell me about yourself.

○ Gives a description based on work experience for mid-career recruitments or school/academic life for students

✕ Fails to understand the question

Tell me about one thing you can do best for the company based on your strengths and your experience. (mid-career)

○ Gives an example of a strength that can be leveraged in your company

✕ Unable to give an answer straightaway

Explain your job history in one minute.

○ Stresses their experience that can be leveraged in the company, within the time limit

✕ Unable to finish their answer within the time limit

[A twist on reasons for leaving]

Did you leave your prior jobs on good terms?

○ Able to confirm that they left their prior jobs on good terms

✕ Describes an unpleasant leaving experience or simply answers 'Yes'

So you left the company because of bad sales. What did you do to improve the situation? (mid-career)

○ Gives a detailed explanation, showing a sense of responsibility

✕ Blames others while answering the question

Explain briefly your reasons for leaving. (mid-career)

○ Gives multiple credible reasons

✕ Leaves an impression that the same thing could happen in your company as well

Standard questions

[Questions for an insight into working ability and aptitude]

Desk jobs:

Why did you choose this job?

○ Has a clear vision of what they want to do

✕ Gives a vague answer that lacks credibility

We sometimes transfer our clerks to the sales department. Are you fine with that?

○ Understands that being flexible is part of contributing to the company and shows respect

✕ Appears unconvinced

What skills do you think are required for a clerical job?

○ Gives an answer based on the understanding of the work type

✕ Unable to answer due to a lack of understanding

Tell me your strengths that can benefit our company.

○ Gives an answer based on the requirements of the job

✕ Gives an answer that lacks relevance to the job

Sales jobs:

Tell me about your strengths as a salesperson. (fresh grads)

○ Gives an answer that shows good research skills and the ability to self-analyze

✕ Gives a vague answer

What type of person do your peers see you as?

○ From the remarks of a third party, have an insight that the applicant has a good relationship with their peers

✕ Unable to picture them having good relationships with others

How can you utilize your experience as a salesperson in our company? (mid-career)

○ Able to describe specific ways of selling

✕ Unable to give a solid answer due to lack of research

Tell me about the difficulties you have experienced as a salesperson. (mid-career)

○ Shows that they have learnt a valuable lesson, providing a credible episode

✕ Gives an episode that lacks credibility or sees the issue negatively

Standard questions —————————————————

Shop assistant and manager jobs:

Have you been to one of our stores?

○ Gives a credible comment on the store

✕ Has not been to the store, or gives an answer lacking credibility

Do you have experience working as a shop manager? (mid-career)

○ Shows that their working ability can be leveraged in the company

✕ Has no experience or gives an answer lacking in credibility

Technical jobs:

How would you utilize the skills you have learnt? (fresh grads)

○ Shows an understanding of the job and that they are passionate about it

✕ Gives a vague answer due to a lack of understanding about the job

Would you mind telling me about your job-hunting situation? (mid-career)

○ Shows an eagerness to join your company as well as putting your company as their first choice

✕ Shows no eagerness to join your company

Where do you want to be in five years' time as a technician?

○ Shows a clear vision of what they want to do in your company

✕ Squeezes out a vague answer

Do you have experience in being a leader? (mid-career)

○ Shows an understanding of and passion for leadership

✕ Has no experience or gives an answer lacking in credibility

Standard questions

Manufacturing jobs:

Why do you want to work in the manufacturing area? (fresh grads)

○ Shows their interest and passion

✕ Gives a vague answer, showing no passion

How do you picture the future of the manufacturing business in Japan?

○ Gives a clear answer

✕ Gives an answer lacking in credibility

Managerial jobs:

Tell me your strengths as a manager and the number of subordinates you have had. (mid-career)

○ Shows strengths that are able to be leveraged in your company

✕ Lacks credibility regarding their managerial experience

Tell me an episode of failure as a manager. (mid-career)

○ Shows that they have learnt from their experience

✕ The experience lacks credibility, or they are transferring responsibility

Standard questions

[Questions for an insight into the applicant's personality by catching them by surprise]

Which do you think is more important: the content of your job or the labor conditions the job offers?

○ Shows a strong passion for their work

✕ Gives an answer lacking in credibility

What will you do when you disagree with your seniors?

○ Answers with the thought of contributing to the company at the back of their minds

✕ Gives an answer lacking in consciousness and credibility

What are your weaknesses at work? (mid-career)

○ Shows the ability to self-analyze and compensate for their weaknesses

✕ Gives an answer lacking in credibility, or fails to self-analyze

What will you do if you do not receive an offer from our company?

○ Shows their passion to continue hunting for the same type of job in the same industry

✕ Lacks thought and vision about what may happen

I believe that you may do well in other job types too. What do you think about that? (mid-career)

○ Shows flexibility, while being passionate about the job they are applying for

✕ Lacks flexibility and stubbornly sticks to the job type they want to do

Is there anyone from this company that you know?

○ Shows that they have a good relationship with a person in the company (if they know anyone)

✕ Stresses how they know each other (if they know anyone)

Standard questions

[Questions for an insight into the applicant's communication skills]

Too bad it is raining today.

○ Able to construct a conversation

✕ The conversation does not last

By the way, what do you do during your spare time?

○ No problem with their lifestyle

✕ Their lifestyle may affect their work performance

How do you relate to people you don't feel comfortable with?

○ Able to construct good relationships

✕ Shows a possibility that they may have trouble dealing with human relationships

Are there things that you bear in mind when talking to your subordinates? (mid-career)

○ Makes solid suggestions based on experience

✕ Gives an answer lacking in credibility

Do you communicate much with people outside the company?

- ○ Shows an active willingness to socialize and communicate with others
- ✕ Shows no interest in socializing or communicating with others

Standard questions

[Questions for an insight into the applicant's ability to accommodate others]

Have you had troubles with human relationships?

○ Shows that they have learnt from their experience

✕ Shows a lack of consciousness to build relationships with others

Are there people at work that you dislike?

○ Gives an understandable answer, showing their belief in the importance of working with all sorts of people

✕ Shows no such belief or gives a stubborn answer

How do you treat a person when you first meet them?

○ Talks about how to build a good relationship with people

✕ Shows a lack of experience or gives an answer lacking in credibility

Have you ever worked as part of a team in the past? (mid-career)

○ Understands the importance of building good teamwork

✕ Lacks experience of teamwork and doesn't seem to understand its importance

What is essential to revitalize an organization? (mid-career)

○ Gives a credible answer based on experience

✕ Shows a lack of consciousness about what works in an organization

What do you think about a young employee becoming your senior? (mid-career)

○ No problem based on experience

✕ Shows signs of disapproval through their facial expressions, even though they may say the opposite

Standard questions

[Questions for an insight into the applicant's sense of responsibility]

Have you experienced troubles in your extracurricular clubs and activities? (fresh grads)

◯ Shows what they have learnt from what they have experienced and know how they can leverage such experiences during work

✕ Transfers responsibilities or only talks about the results

Can you tell me an episode of failure from your working experience? (mid-career)

◯ Shows that they have learnt from their mistakes

✕ Fails to identify it as a failure or transfers responsibility

What is the difference between casual workers and full-time workers? (mid-career)

◯ Shows an understanding of working full-time

✕ Talks about stability or other factors based on themselves

What do you think "responsibility" means when applied to this job? (mid-career)

○ Gives an understandable and credible answer

✕ Gives a stereotyped answer that lacks credibility

How do you react when things are not going your way? (mid-career)

○ Able to self-analyze and finds a way to solve the problem

✕ Gives a vague answer lacking in credibility

Standard questions ——————————————————

[Questions for an insight into the applicant's stress tolerance]

How do you deal with stress?

○ Has a set of ways to deal with stress

✕ Has not thought about it, thus unable to answer the question

How do you change your mood when things are not going as planned? (mid-career)

○ Shows a tolerance to stress

✕ Unable to give an answer on the spot; may have problems with managing stress

It seems that you have only been talking about your part-time working experience. What about your studies? (fresh grads)

○ Humbly accepts negatives that are pointed out and talks about how they can improve the situation

✕ Starts giving excuses

You have been changing jobs very frequently. Are you going to change jobs soon this time as well? (mid-career pressure interview)

○ Does not deny the fact pointed out and shows their desire for greater stability in the future

✕ Starts to panic and gives a vague answer

The blank period since you left your last workplace has been long. Are you sure you are still capable of working? (mid-career pressure interview)

○ Confident because they have been using the time on self-development

✕ Seems concerned

Standard questions

[Questions for an insight into the applicant's enthusiasm for working in a field where they lack experienced]

Have you ever done any self-development training?

- ◯ Gives evidence that they have upgraded relevant skills on their own time
- ✕ Has done nothing, or nothing credible

Why are you applying for an entry-level position? (mid-career)

- ◯ Has a strong will to work in the area, and their explanation is understandable
- ✕ Gives a vague answer, leaving others confused about what the applicant is thinking about

Are you okay with young supervisors? (mid-career)

- ◯ Shows a strong will to be part of the workforce
- ✕ Shows a concerned face and gives an answer lacking in credibility

Your wages will be much less than you have been getting. Are you fine with that? (mid-career)

○ Shows eagerness and confidence in working

✕ Expression changes and does not seem convinced

Tell me about your vision for the future. (mid-career)

○ Shows an understanding of the job type they are inexperienced in

✕ Gives a vague answer due to lack of understanding

Standard questions

[Questions one hesitates to ask]

What do you think about working in the future? (mid-career)

○ Shows strong will to continue working in the future

✕ Gives a vague answer and seems concerned

What would you do if your partner were to be transferred to a different workplace? (mid-career)

○ Their partner has an understanding of their job and thus the applicant is able to work in the future

✕ Unable to give a clear answer

What would you do if your child were to fall ill? (mid-career)

○ Has the support of their partner and extended family

✕ Has no specific plans

Can you balance work and life? (mid-career)

○ Has discussed this with their partner and there is no problem

✕ Gives an answer lacking in credibility

Are you okay with overnight business trips away from home? (mid-career)

○ Has no problem

✕ Seems concerned or gives a vague answer

Employment situation in Japan

Fresh graduates: Job-hunting

In Japan, job-hunting begins from about the third year of university, although in recent times some universities have started offering classes in job-hunting to first-year students.

During summer vacation, students research companies where they want to work, looking at job offers at the university and on the Internet. They participate in a lot of information sessions designed to inform them about each company's business results and activities, in preparation for job interviews.

Some companies look for students who would like to work as interns.

Most graduates undergo a number of interviews for each position. Interviewers ask applicants why they want to work at the company. They are asked to share their interests and to self-assess their value to the company. Many companies also have written tests or aptitude tests.

As high-school graduates are mostly inexperienced, more is made of their potential. They choose from job offers in the high school and apply to the company through the recommendation of the high school.

Interview procedure is formal. At each interview, fresh grads knock on the door, enter the room and stand beside a chair. They state their name and the name of the university that they will graduate from, and then sit down, sitting up straight in the chair. They are judged on their manner and personality as well as their university results. After several interviews it is decided whether to pass or fail the applicant.

Mid-career applicants: Changing jobs

Mid-career applicants find new jobs through job offers on the Internet, official employment bureaus, or employment agencies. The company interviews each applicant a number of times, making much of the applicant's manner and personality as well as evaluating business skills. The decision about whether to pass or fail the applicant is usually made after several interviews, but sometimes the company decides to employ the applicant after just one interview.

As with fresh grads, the interview is important, though some companies also place importance on the applicant's résumé, written tests, and aptitude tests.

Mid-career applicants are expected to become suitable workers in a short timeframe.

Papers to turn in

Fresh grads turn in a résumé and an entry sheet. Mid-career applicants turn in a résumé and a CV. Both usually buy a typed pro forma résumé at a stationery shop or convenience store, or download it from the Internet. They write their address, name, phone number, educational background and qualifications on the form.

Though most CVs are typed, a lot of companies still recommend handwritten forms. Even if applicants apply online, many companies expect them to also submit a paper résumé also.

Permanent employment still the cultural climate of Japan

Job turnover in Japan is more volatile than it used to be. Data show that 70% of fresh high-school graduates, 50% of fresh college graduates and 30% of fresh university graduates quit the job in three years. Nonetheless, permanent employment, even if less than before, still is the cultural norm in Japan. Fresh grads are 'grown' over the long term in this climate. As well as job skills and results, loyalty and a sense of belonging to the company are regarded as important, and employees' careers are nurtured through frequent job rotation.

At one time, some Japanese companies introduced an annual income system, but a pro-results employment system didn't take root. Some companies have been changing their employment systems back to earlier systems that offered employees a retirement allowance. Therefore at the interviews, companies tend to evaluate the applicant's loyalty to the company, for example through asking them why they prefer the company to other companies.

AFTERWORD

Recently, a customer service manager said that they mainly conducted pressure interviews when recruiting fresh graduates. They conducted harsh interviews aimed at hiring people who could tolerate customer complaints. I heard that some applicants ended up in tears. Such interviews are total nonsense and a great shame.

I do not believe in harsh interviews where interviewers belittle their applicants and hire only those who have survived the harsh pressure tournament, especially for customer services. Although you might gain an insight into the stress tolerance of the applicant through a pressure interview, I cannot say it is the right thing to do when considering the burden it puts on the applicant. If stress tolerance is an important factor you would like to focus on, you can gain an insight through aptitude tests and questions about stress tolerance. Also, I think that it is more important that someone from the service industry knows how to please a customer, rather than tolerate customer complaints. I do not think that the applicants who fail the test will ever use the services of that company. I also doubt that those who survive the harsh test and receive an offer will stay in the company for long.

In interview environments, it is not the interviewer who has the upper hand. Both the applicant and company have the right to choose. While the interviewer gets an insight into the applicant and judges if they are right for their company, the applicant is also gaining an insight into the company, deciding if it is worth spending their life there. The judgment of the interviewer literally changes lives. Interviews based purely on technique will not allow the applicant's voice to be heard. Mismatching will occur if judgments are superficial.

Each interview is a serious game between the interviewer and the applicant. They are seeing if they can speak what they think to each other within a short space of time.

To those who have read this book, please conduct each interview as though it will be remembered by each applicant for the rest of their lives. I can still recall the words and facial expressions of the interviewers who interviewed me during a fresh grad recruitment after all these years. I remember wanting so badly to work in that company after the interview—just because of the gentle eyes of the interviewer and the attitude of listening to every word I said.

Interviews are not just about experience and techniques. Please put this book into practice, ask questions that would draw out the applicants' real intentions, and observe not only their words, but also the applicants' facial expressions and attitude. Then be sure to welcome the newly hired as one of you, and give them an environment in which they will be able to spread their wings and soar. Recruitment does not end after finding the right person. Helping them build a path to walk on is also the job of recruitment personnel.

I wish, from the bottom of my heart, that you will be able to find the right people and that your company will flourish.

Kenichiro Yadokoro

Author's
profile

Kenichiro Yadokoro

CEO of Career Domain, Co. Ltd.
http://cdomain.jp

A member of Japan Career Development Association, Career development advisor (CDA)

Yadokoro studied overseas in a state high school in New York while attending the University of Tokyo Secondary School attached to the Faculty of Education. After his graduation from Musashi University with an economics degree, he started working for Yanase & Co. and then moved to Socie World Co. where he was involved in recruitment activities. In Tsunahachi Corporation. he became an experienced HR manager. Since then he has been working free-lance in the field of recruitment. He offers sample interviews to job-hunters and a HR consultancy, and has lectured on recruitment to more than ten thousand people.